Keys to Successful Mentoring Relationships

By

Dr. Mary J. Ogenaarekhua

Endorsements

*"In **Keys to Successful Mentoring Relationships,** Dr. Mary Ogenaarekhua clearly outlines keys to building meaningful and productive mentoring relationships using easy to apply guidelines regardless of whether you are mentoring others or seeking someone to mentor you. These focused methods define the art of mentoring and they maximize the benefits of mentoring whether utilized in the Christian, business, educational or parenting arena. This textbook truly lays a solid foundation for those desiring to effectively impart their wisdom and talents to others or receive what others have to impart to them."*

—**Lynne Garbinsky**

Dedication

As in my other books, I dedicate this book to God the Father, God the Son and God the Holy Ghost. Lord God, You gave me the words to write in this book and I give You all the glory. As it is written in **Psalms 68:11**, so You have done concerning this book:

> *"The Lord gave the word: great was the company of those that published it."*

Thanks Father for mentoring me and teaching me how to mentor others. You are truly a great teacher and You are the best! It is a great honor to be mentored by You.

Again, I thank You for giving me **To His Glory Publishing Company**. You have made it a great company. Father, to You be all the glory.

I also dedicate this book to all the students in my mentoring class.

Keys to Successful Mentoring Relationships

Most of the scriptures are quoted from the King James and the New International Versions of the Bible

Mary's Purpose: To provide a place for you to demonstrate integrity so that wisdom and compassion are realized for commitment to fulfill your God-given purpose.

Published by: **To His Glory Publishing Company, Inc.**
463 Dogwood Drive, NW
Lilburn, GA 30047
(770) 458-7947
www.tohisglorypublishing.com
www.maryjministries.org
email: tohisglorypublishing@yahoo.com

Book is available at:
Amazon.com, BarnesandNoble.com, Borders.com, Booksamillion.com, etc.
Book is also available in UK and Canada

www.tohisglorypublishing.com
(770) 458-7947

ISBN: 978-0-9791566-6-3   or   0-9791566-6-1

Table of Contents

Preface

There are people in Christendom that demonstrate the character and the ways of the Lord and when we see such people, we are immediately drawn to them. They demonstrate faithfulness, integrity, honesty, love, compassion, mercy, etc. We admire them and observe the way they conduct themselves or the intelligence that they display and we want to walk up to them to compliment them. Some of us want to approach them because we want to learn from them the things that we have noticed and admired in them. This is called "mentoring" in Christendom and "coaching" in the workplace. Some people never summon the courage to approach such people while some have approached the people and they enjoyed a very rewarding and fulfilling mentoring relationship. There are also those who have been disappointed by the response that they received or the reaction of the person they approached.

Whatever have been your previous experiences, this book is designed to help you approach mentoring in a godly way that will minimize your disappointment and eliminate any hidden fears or apprehensions. God's commandment to us through the Apostle Paul in **2 Timothy 2:2** is:

> **"And the things that thou hast heard of me among many witnesses, the same commit thou to faithful men, <u>who shall be able to teach others also</u>."**

It is God's will that the older men and women teach the younger ones. This is one effective way that godly principles are passed on. What I have discovered in Christendom is that most people do not genuinely know how to go about mentoring another person and they do not know what is involved in a mentoring relationship.

This book is therefore intended to help both the would-be-mentor and "mentee" (the person to be mentored) to better understand the dynamics in a mentor/mentee relationship. It outlines what is involved in this type of relationship and what each party in the relationship should expect. A mentor/mentee relationship is not to be entered into lightly. Just like any other human relationship, it can leave the parties with a feeling of rejection, abandonment and resentment if not handled properly.

There is a saying that the mark of a good teacher is reflected in the quality of the students the teacher produces. **Philippians 4:9** states:

> **"Those things, which ye have both
> learned, and received, and heard,
> and seen in me, do: and the God
> of peace shall be with you."**

Mentoring gives us the opportunity to teach others what the Lord has graciously bestowed on us. It gives us the opportunity to use our talents for the Lord's glory.

Acknowledgements

I extend my gratitude to all the students in my mentoring class for their support and participation in the mentoring program.

I would like to acknowledge all the people that encouraged me to develop these materials for mentoring.

I also thank those that have come to me with requests for mentoring relationships. Thank you for placing a demand on me concerning mentoring. I pray that this workbook will be beneficial to us all. God bless you.

Questions about Mentoring Relationships

I remember the first time I went up to someone about mentoring me and how she turned to me and asked, "What exactly do you see in me?" She laughed and I waited for her to get back to me after she has had time to pray and think about my request. I never heard from her and I did not approach her again on the subject. It just died.

When I reflected on the matter some years later, I realized that neither she nor I knew how to go about establishing a mentoring relationship. I knew that she liked me and as I watched her, it became clear to me that she genuinely did not know what to do with me concerning mentoring. Just like her, I did not know how to pursue the relationship either.

We both needed to find out what mentoring was all about. I needed to have done some homework on the subject and she also needed to know what was involved in mentoring. We were both ignorant of what mentoring is about and we needed God's guidance on the matter.

In retrospect, I can see where we both made our mistakes. To begin with, I did not pray about my request and I do not think she did either. Without the Lord, we cannot do anything. He is the one that gives us wisdom about what we are supposed to do and how we are supposed to do it.

The following are some of the questions that I have asked myself over the years and that I think you may need to answer before pursuing a mentoring relationship. Answers to these questions will help prepare you for seeking and establishing a successful mentoring relationship.

- *What is a mentor?*
- *What is a mentee?*
- *Do I need a mentor?*
- *Why do I need a mentor?*
- *What is involved in a mentor/mentee relationship?*
- *Who needs a mentor?*
- *What is the difference between a mentor and a counselor?*
- *Do I still need a mentor when I have a pastor?*
- *How do I go about finding a mentor?*
- *What do I expect from my mentor?*
- *What do I expect from my mentee?*
- *How long is a mentoring relationship?*
- *How do I know when to let go when the season of mentoring is over?*

Note: *The materials in this book were first presented in actual classroom settings.*

Chapter 1

Identifying Reasons for Needing Mentoring

In this particular chapter on identifying reasons for needing mentoring, I want to stress that it is a privilege to be properly instructed on how to be mentored and how to mentor others. This is essential because as you are being mentored, you are also learning how to pass on to others the things that you have learned that are based on the spiritual gifts that God has given you. The things you learn from your mentor will help you to get established in the gifts and calling of God upon your life. They will help you to develop self confidence and to boldly step out in the anointing upon your life.

As this begins to happen, others are going to find the godly qualities that you demonstrate attractive and at one point, they are going to come up to you and say to you, "You know what? I would like to learn from you; I would like to partner with you and I would like for you to be my coach and to be my mentor because you demonstrate godly character." When this happens, it would not be the time for you to begin to want to find out what mentoring is all about or what the dynamics of a successful mentoring relationship are. This is why I am presenting the materials in this book in a classroom approach so that you can sit down and be properly mentored as well as have a one-on-one mentoring relationship with your mentor.

As I stated above, some of the things that may happen is that somebody might come up to you and say to you, "I want you to mentor me or I want you to be my coach." For example, I was speaking to a young man recently and he said to me, "A guy just came to me and wanted me to be his mentor and I do not know what I am supposed to do with the guy." I said to him, "Most people feel exactly the way that you feel because when somebody comes up to us or when we go to somebody about mentoring, most of us do not really know what to do."

Laying the Basic Foundation:
I will begin here by laying the vital foundation about God's all-important agenda in His dealings with man. You see, God set out in **Genesis 1:26** to make a specimen –a being that He called man. He had in His heart a blue print of this specimen that He desires and He outlined it. He stated what He wants this being (man) to look like and to be like as it is written:

> **"And God said, <u>Let us make man in our image</u>, <u>after our likeness</u>: and let them have dominion over the fish of the sea, and over the fowl of the air, and over the cattle, and over all the earth, and over every creeping thing that creepeth upon the earth."**

This is God's critical blueprint. Before somebody builds a house, the person has to decide beforehand, if it is going to be a one-story, two-story or three-story building that he or she desires. The person also has to decide how many rooms he or she wants in the house and what this house is going to be like. Therefore, the person gets an architect to come up with a blueprint for the house. The architect will then carefully draw the blueprint with specific details and the builder will then make sure that when the house is finished, it looks just like the blueprint.

Now, God set out in the beginning to make a man and He had a definite idea of what He wants; a man that does not just look like Him but has His character! You have heard the saying, "Like father, like son." This is exactly what God is saying to us in **Genesis 1:26**—"Let us make man in our image after our likeness." Because God has this blue print or specimen in mind, He takes a very personal interest in us. Therefore, when we come to God the Father through His Son, Jesus Christ, He begins the process of conforming us to the image of His Son because of the blueprint that He outlined from the very beginning. **The reason He conforms us to Christ is because the Lord Jesus Christ is the only person that has perfectly exhibited the image of God the Father and has perfectly exhibited the character of God the Father.** So, when God seeks to conform us to His Son, it is for a purpose. It is because Jesus is the walking specimen of the blueprint that God the Father outlined in **Genesis 1:26**—making a man that does not just look like Him but will perfectly exhibit His character and faithfully represent Him wherever He goes.

When you look at the compliment He gave to David, you will see Him making a reference to the specimen in **Genesis 1:26**. What did He call David? He said David is, "A man after my own heart that will do all my will." In other words, David would faithfully represent Me. Therefore, it is critical that when we come to Christ that we do not just learn to talk the talk but we must also to learn to walk the walk. If there is an area in which you are talking the talk but you are not able to walk the walk, you should cry out for help to someone that you see "walking right" in that area.

One way to ask for help is through the avenue of mentoring. You need someone who will be instrumental in God's hand in helping to "conform you" to the image of Christ because at the end, when God looks at you and me, He will be looking for a man (women included) that is in His image and after His likeness. In other words, He will be looking for a man that has His character and acts just like Him!

God has not changed His **Genesis 1:26** blueprint. That it why the Word says, **"Do not be deceived, God is not mocked"** (Galatians 6:7). So, when He says in the New Testament that we are to be conformed and that we are to be transformed, this is what He is taking about. We must be like Christ and what happens to us when we come to the Lord is that we are expected to grow. And as we grow in Christ, there are some of us that have a very good handle on scriptures and some of us do not. In other words, some of us can recall scriptures real easy while some of us do not remember scriptures. What happens then is that those who have been established; those whom God has worked in their lives and has established in some area can be of help to those who are new or young in the kingdom. For instance, in a mentoring situation, there are some people whose knowledge of scriptures are limited and therefore might need to be referred to a group that has a very good handle on Bible study so that they can learn scriptures.

If after talking to your new mentee you discover that he or she needs to be challenged in their knowledge of scriptures, you can refer them to a good Bible study group. **The reason you need to have a good knowledge of the Word of God is because you can never grow above the knowledge of the Word of God that is in you.** This is why you must really spend time in the Word because the level of the Word of God that is inside of you determines the extent of your growth spiritually and physically. The scripture in **3 John 1:2** says:

> **"Beloved, I wish above all things that <u>thou mayest prosper and be in health, even as thy soul prospereth</u>."**

<u>Therefore, if your soul is not prospering in the Word of God and in the ways of God, do not look for prosperity in the physical because your physical prosperity is tied with the spiritual prosperity of your soul.</u> You have to be willing to really take a look; to take a realistic appraisal of yourself when it comes to mentoring and say, "God, I don't want to mock you so conform me to the image of Your Son so that I can become the person that You started out to make." I want you to be pleased with me at the end of this world because I am conformed to the image of Your Son. When I saw in **Genesis 6:6** that "it grieved God at His heart" for having made man, I chose to be one that will bless His heart always. I chose to let God do His work in me so that I can be what He has made and called me to be.

> **"And it <u>repented the LORD that he had made man</u> on the earth, and <u>it grieved him at his heart</u>."**

Yes, in the days of Noah, God destroyed all living beings except Noah and his family because He regretted having created man. I thought that this was very serious because the Bible says that it grieved God in His heart. It did not just grieve Him but it grieved Him in His heart and God repented for having made man. When I read this, I said to the Lord, "I don't ever want to be one of those people that You look at and You say, 'It grieves Me for having made this one.' But

I want to be one that brings praise and glory to Your name and joy to Your heart." If you read **Isaiah 43:21**, you will see that God's heart desire is that we live for the praise and glory of His name:

> **"This people have I formed for myself; they shall shew forth my praise."**

Therefore, you should be a living and walking testimony of the goodness of God to those who see you and the prosperity of God, the love of God and mercy of God should flow through you in every place you go. You should be a "living epistle of Christ" no matter what you are going through because you always overcome even in the worst situation. People should always have a reason to say, "Praise the Lord" whenever they have an encounter with you. This is how He wants us to walk in our Christian life.

Mentoring is needed in the body of Christ because those in the body of Christ who are not able to apprehend the ways of God can be helped through mentoring. Such people need somebody to guide them. Mentoring allows you to take what God has placed within you by *hearing His voice* to help another person until the person is at a point where he or she can hear His voice or know His ways. No one can place the call of God within you. The call of God upon your life is before you were born and the gifts of God that are in you are in you for good. God does not give and take away but He wants you to mature and to be a vessel that He can use. God does not want us to remain babes forever. He loves to see us grow and one of the ways that our Christian growth is accomplished is mentoring—the older ones helping the younger ones!

Those who are well seasoned in the Lord must be willing to be used by the Lord to raise up the younger generation. We have to make ourselves accessible to the Lord to use for His glory. Some people are too busy in their daily schedule that they are not available when the Lord needs to use them even in the little things. Below is a story that tells us all how the Lord feels about it.

"One day, I was on Buford Highway in Georgia and I went to the Wachovia bank at the corner of Buford Highway and I-285/ I-85 north. When I got to the door of the bank, I found a note that said that the bank was closed for some kind of a holiday so I purposely avoided this bank for about two years. Would you believe that when I went back to this same bank on another day after two years that I again got to the front door of the bank only to find a note that said that the bank was closed for another kind of holiday? I said to myself, 'Wait a minute, there is something wrong with this picture because twice I have come over here now in two years plus and twice I have found a note that said that the bank was closed.'

I was a little upset as I was driving away and it turned out to be one of those little things that make you feel sorry for yourself and so I was feeling a little sorry for myself. While I was in that state, the Lord said to me, 'I too am looking for banks that are open' and I said, 'What do you mean? He said, 'My children, they are open when they want something from Me but when I come to make a withdrawal of the gifts

*and anointing that I placed within them, I also
get a note that says that they are closed.'"*

I learned from this experience and interaction with the
Lord that we have to be willing to impart to other people
those things that the Lord has put within us because the
spiritual law is to give in order to receive. If God teaches
you a principle today and you run and tell somebody, you
will be surprised at how quickly He will add to what He
has given you because He knows that you are not a closed
bank. He knows that when He comes to make a withdrawal,
there will not be a notice that you are closed. He can always
put somebody in your path and trust you to say something
to them, to give them a word of encouragement or just to
represent Him before that person. When God begins to use
you this way, people will continually ask you, "Why are you
always the one meeting the people in need and having these
unique experiences?" It is because when you step out, God
lines up the people for you to have a divine encounter with.
This is how it works; as you give, you receive more and
more. If you are waiting to be all put together and wrapped
up with a bow that says "all done and you are perfect" before
you feel like you are worthy to help somebody else, then
something is wrong and as far as God is concerned, you are
a closed bank.

We need to look and see even in the body of Christ,
the people that need our help. There are some people that
you see and they come to church and you look at them and
go, "Didn't their mother tell them about how they looked
before they left the house, didn't somebody in the house
say something to them about how they looked before they
walked out of the house?" You see people walking about
in the church looking like slobs, drifters and vagabonds and
nobody says anything because mentoring is lacking.

When the Lord opens the door for you to be able to help such people, do not be a closed bank. Mentoring involves looking at somebody; looking at the totality of the person versus the specimen that God outlined in **Genesis 1:26.** You do not want to be one that runs around thinking that you are in right standing with the Lord only to find yourself a cast away at the end. Mentoring helps to conform you to God's original specimen that according to His specification is fit to enter into His heaven. It is possible to live an unholy life while preaching the gospel to others or to walk in self-righteousness instead of the righteousness of God in Christ. Your mentor will always hold you accountable and you should also hold yourself accountable in the fear of the Lord. This is why Paul said in **1 Corinthians 9:27**:

> **"But <u>I keep under my body, and bring it into subjection: lest that by any means, when I have preached to others, I myself should be a castaway</u>."**

None of us wants to be a cast away after we have preached to others. Therefore, our walk must line up with the Word that comes out of our mouth according to the Word of God. **I know that some people believe that "once saved always saved" but we can see from the above scripture that you can still be a castaway when your walk does not line up with your talk. The reason is because your life demonstrates to God that you are nothing but a hypocrite.** This is also why the Bible admonishes us through Paul in **Titus 2:1-10** as follows:

> **"But speak thou the things which become <u>sound doctrine</u>: <u>That the aged men be sober, grave, temperate, sound in faith, in charity,</u>**

in patience. The aged women
likewise, that they be in behaviour
as becometh holiness, not false
accusers, not given to much wine,
teachers of good things; That they
may teach the young women to be
sober, to love their husbands, to
love their children, To be discreet,
chaste, keepers at home, good,
obedient to their own husbands,
that the word of God be not
blasphemed. Young men likewise
exhort to be sober minded. In all
things shewing thyself a pattern of
good works: in doctrine shewing
uncorruptness, gravity, sincerity,
Sound speech, that cannot be
condemned; that he that is of the
contrary part may be ashamed,
having no evil thing to say of you.
Exhort servants to be obedient
unto their own masters, and to
please them well in all things; not
answering again; Not purloining,
but shewing all good fidelity; that
they may adorn the doctrine of
God our Saviour in all things."

You will see in the above scripture, the characteristics of
godly qualities that we as Christians ought to possess. For
example, there should not be a brawl and guess who is in the
midst of it—you, because you are not to be quick tempered.
You should not be a person who does not have faith and does
not walk in love. You are not to be full of judgment against
people. You can tell when somebody is judgmental, all you

have to do is just spend five minuets with the person and their judgmental attitude comes out in every statement the person makes about others.

The Bible is telling us in this particular scripture what godly qualities are. If someone should come up to you and ask you, "What are the qualities of a godly person?" This is a good scripture to use in your response. It helps you to know the qualities of a godly person that we are all expected to posses and you can use these qualities to measure yourself in order to see how well you are doing as a Christian. According to this scripture, a godly man is sound in faith, very patient, temperate and sober —**"That the aged men be sober, grave, temperate, sound in faith, in charity, in patience…Young men likewise exhort to be sober minded."** It also says that godly women are to exhibit behavior that demonstrates holiness—**"the aged women likewise, that they be in behaviour as becometh holiness."** Remember that Jesus told us through Paul that without holiness "no man shall see God." The reason for this is because righteousness is given to us as a gift when we become born again. We do not have to do anything to earn righteousness but just believe that God the Father sent God the Son to pay for our sins. That faith in the finished work of Christ is counted to us as righteousness. God expunged all our sins; He wiped them out and declared us justified (righteous), unblameable and unreproveable in His sight (**Colossians 1:22**). It was given to us because we believed.

Now, holiness is something that is different. Holiness requires that you sanctify yourself and that you purposely withdraw yourself from all things that might defile you. Holiness requires that you avoid all things that would be dishonoring to God and that you avoid all things that are outright sin. It means that if you are married, you will be faithful and you do not flirt with the opposite sex and then say, "Well, I did not do anything unfaithful with him or her, I just flirted." It is still a spirit of lust and unfaithfulness that you are playing around with. You cannot lie, cheat and steal and just because you didn't get caught, feel that everything is OK. You now have the Holy Spirit within you and He will bring you in line by putting a check in your spirit if you let Him. For example, if you used to have a habit of picking up things that did not belong to you, when you stretch out your hand in an attempt to pick up something that belongs to another person, the Holy Spirit will say to you, "We don't do that anymore so put it back." Or if you took it home, the Holy Spirit will not leave you alone until you take it back to the store or find a way to sneak it back to the place where it belongs.

Something in you has got to change as a result of having the Holy Spirit dwell in you. We are not to be false accusers and we are not to be drunkards. The Bible tells us not to drink too much wine but to be teachers of good things. Again,

> **"The aged women likewise, that they be in behaviour as becometh holiness, not false accusers, not given to much wine, teachers of good things"** (Titus 2:3).

This is why most mentoring books will tell you that we are to teach the younger women how to be sober, to love their husbands, to love their children, to be discrete, chaste, to be keepers of good homes and obedient to their own husbands so that the Word of God may not be blasphemed. These things are not just limited to the wife only. The husband has to do his part to be chaste and take care of his household as well. He has to honor his wife and not put her down or belittle her or her household duties. Everything that the woman is required to do; the husband is also required to do as well.

We are to be examples of the believers to all those who observe us on a daily basis. We are not to give occasion to unbelievers to reproach us and our God by saying, "I thought they were Christians" and then have another unbeliever reply, "That's what they all say."

> *When I was working at a large shipping company, I remember another lady who was also a believer in my department and I thought we were on the same side because we were Christians. Some of the unbelievers used to go to a strip club to eat lunch. She thought there was nothing wrong with it and I said I was not going to dabble with the spirit of stripping whether there were ladies dancing on the pole or not. If I was not going for the sole purpose of soul winning; even then, it will be on the outside, I will not be found there. I told them that if I go there, it will be by the direction of the Holy Spirit telling me to go get someone out. I told this colleague of mine that I was not going to sit down there and fellowship with the establishment and then tomorrow expect to be able to cast out the demons in there or help a lady that is struggling in that area of her life. She did not see anything wrong with it and the next thing I knew she started going out with these people in the evenings on Fridays.*

> *One Monday afternoon, I was sitting at the lunch table in the lunch room and she was not there. A guy, whom I can tell has a lifestyle that was contrary to the teachings of the Bible, was sitting with a lady across from*

me. Their conversation went something like this, "Didn't you see so and so (they called her name; the Christian lady) dancing and just throwing down like anyone of us at the party on Saturday?" The lady that he was sitting with replied, "Yah, and I thought she said she was a Christian." The guy replied, "Well, that's what they all say." It was obvious that they were saying these things for me to hear and they tried hard to get me into the conversation but I made up my mind that I was not going to get involved in their Christian bashing. But, before the Christian started running around with them, I told her not go with them and bring reproach on the name of the Lord, but she did not listen. To make matters worse, the very person that she thought was on her side turned around a week later and fired her. The same week, one of the ladies came to me and said, "If I ever decide to be a Christian, I want to be your kind of Christian." I said to her, "What do you mean?" and she said, "Because you don't compromise; what you preach is what you do."

There are many ways that you can be a witness without even doing anything. We are to make sure that the name of God and the Word of God are not blasphemed. Now, the scripture talks about exhorting —**"the young men likewise exhort to be sober minded. In all things shewing thyself a pattern of good works: in doctrine:"** See how it goes back to what you believe? What you believe matters a lot because if you believe wrong, you are going to act wrong. Your beliefs control your actions.

Our words and behavior must line up with God's Word so that unbelievers do not reproach us and our God. This is why we are told the following. **"...Shewing uncorruptness, gravity, sincerity, Sound speech, that cannot be condemned; that he that is of the contrary part** *(unbelievers)* **may be ashamed, having no evil thing to say of you."** You should always leave "a legacy of the believer" everywhere you go. Even while you are still at the place, you might be surprised that when those unbelievers want something or are in crisis, they know who to go to for prayer. They might judge you for being too firm in your Christian belief or for not compromising, but when things go wrong, guess who they are going to call—you! They will call you to the corner and ask, "Can you pray for me?" This is why you must always leave good things such a legacy, behavior, reputation, etc., behind you wherever you go. When you leave a place, there should be a legacy that shows or speaks to the fact that there was once a person that worked there or that sat in a particular cube and the person was a true man or woman of God. **They will testify that you did not compromise and that you held onto what you believed.**

The scripture further instructs us to **"Exhort servants to be obedient unto their own masters, and to please them well in all things; not answering again;"** In other words, do not say negative things back to your master or your boss. There are times when you should just let the Lord deal with a particular situation on your behalf. You don't have to prove that you are right or that they are wrong but just let the Lord deal with it for you. God is not looking for who is right or wrong; God is looking for who is obedient and humble.

"Not purloining, but shewing all good fidelity; that they may adorn the doctrine of God our Saviour in all

things." In other words, you are not to take that which belongs to another as I stated before and you are to let the Word of God guide you in everything that you do. Adopt a Christ-like attitude and behavior in all that you do. Be committed and faithful to do what you have been given to do.

I will again re-emphasize what the main scripture in this chapter is exhorting us to do. God expects us to impart to the younger generation or to the people that come to us, the things that we have learned from Him. The older women are to teach the younger women and the older men are to teach the younger men. Passing on knowledge is needed in the body of Christ today so that the younger generation can be established in godly behavior and beliefs. If you look at the Jewish custom, you will see that this is how God also taught them to pass on knowledge to the younger generations. Therefore, you are supposed to pass knowledge on to your children and you are supposed to pass it on to those that are within your sphere of influence.

We are to emulate those who are walking godly as we observe their behavior and when they speak into our lives, we are to follow their counsel. That is why the Apostle Paul was bold enough to say, **"Be ye followers of me, even as I also am of Christ"** (1 Corinthians 11:1). He had made a decision that he was going to perfectly exhibit the Lord's character in everything that he did. He counted everything as dung for the purpose of knowing Christ, walking according to the Word of God and letting the Word of God dominate everything that he did. He chose to walk all the days of his life according to the principles of the Word of God because he was totally sold out to God.

Mentor/Mentoring Defined:
At this point, I think that it is good for me to <u>formally</u>

address what it means to be in a mentoring relationship. **The dictionary refers to the mentor as a wise trusted teacher or counselor.** That is the dictionary definition but for our purpose, we need to know that sometimes your mentor may not be a trained or ordained counselor. Some people are taught or mentored by their counselor so it important for us to know that the dictionary just kind of lumped a teacher and a counselor together in its definition. The mentor is the one who instructs.

Sometimes, your mentor is just somebody who is exhibiting the qualities of a true man or woman of God and as you look at him or her, you can see that he or she is flowing in the things that you know that God is calling you to do. Therefore, mentors are people who go before you to pave the way for you to come behind them so you do not have to re-invent the wheel. You can facilitate your spiritual growth by lining up or teaming up with them to be mentored. You may even assist them in their ministries so that you could learn some of the things that might save you from accomplishing your ministry the hard way.

A mentoring relationship begins when two or more people agree to begin a teaching or training relationship in which the "mentor" (teacher) imparts to the "mentee" (student or trainee), attributes or qualities that the mentor possesses. The mentor is therefore the one who teaches the student that which the student has come to learn from him or her. When people hang around you, they will receive or begin to partake of the grace of God that is upon you. Therefore, when people come up to you for mentoring, you need to be honest when telling them the areas in which you can help them. For instance, those who hang around me will tell you that my primary gifts are: seeing, ability to interpret visions and dreams, spiritual discernment, spiritual impartation, healing, deliverance, intercession and knowledge of the Word of God. Some people struggle to understand scriptures but I was not one of such people because as soon as I became born again and began to study the Word, God helped me by enabling me to know His Word. My pastor was amazed at how scriptures seemed to just pour out of my mouth and how the anointing was flowing through me.

I love the Word of God and as a result, when someone approaches me for mentoring, and after an interaction with the person, I can tell almost immediately the depth of the person's knowledge of the Word of God. Also, with most people, I can tell when someone is just "making it through" (pretending to know more than they really do) without a good understanding of the Word of God. What I look for in a person, is the extent of the person's knowledge of the Word of God and how faithful the person is to obey the Word of God. I can discern when someone has been exposed to the healing or deliverance ministry and I can discern when someone is ignorant of what goes on in the realm of the spirit. This type of discernment enables me to know the area that a person needs my help as I proceed to mentor the person. I do not ignore my discernment.

When you are approached for a mentoring relationship and you agree to it, then it is critical that you know the attributes that you as the mentor already possess. You must be true to yourself as to what you know and do not know or what you can do and what you cannot do for your mentee. For instance, I flow in the teaching anointing and you can see as you go further in reading this book that it is laid out in a classroom setting and that you are being taught from a classroom perspective. The reason is because you may be in a church where you have to teach or properly instruct people on how to mentor at the same time that you are mentoring them. I believe that this will also help the students so that when they start a one-on-one mentoring relationship with someone, they are not going to be ignorant about what mentoring is about. They will at least know how to handle the relationship or know what to expect in the relationship. This book is designed to give them a blueprint from which to operate and they can add additional revelation from the Lord to it as they grow.

Mentee Defined:

You are going to hear me refer to the student as the **"mentee"** all through this book. The mentee is someone who is being trained, taught or instructed by another person for the purpose of being raised up spiritually and physically to demonstrate godly character as well as the good attributes of the mentor. As I stated earlier on, you first need to identify some of the reasons why you need another person to mentor you or some of the reasons why you need to mentor another person. This is necessary before embarking on a mentoring relationship.

Mentoring is a very specific assignment and you need to define the reasons in order to be able to set your goals so that at the end, you can determine if the mentoring relationship was successful or not. Both the mentor and the mentee should be able to state at the end of the relationship the things that they learned and determine if it moved them from one level of development to another.

A Mini Exercise

Please take a piece of paper and identify some of the reasons why you need mentoring and if one of the reasons is to be able to mentor other people, write a second set of reasons why you think God is calling you to mentor other people. Identify the type of people that you are called to mentor.

I want to re-emphasize that when you are able to identify the reasons needing mentoring, it helps you to set mentoring goals and it will help you to determine at the end if the goals were met or not. This list will also help you to know what areas you need to be challenged in as a mentee or what areas to challenge others in as you are mentoring them.

Just like the first scripture we read in **Titus 2:1-10**, the following scripture also instructs us to commit to others the things that we have learned so that they can in turn pass the knowledge on.

> **"And the things that thou hast heard of me among many witnesses, the same commit thou to faithful men, who shall be able to teach others also"** (2 Timothy 2:2).

As I stated before, the spiritual principle is to give to others as the Lord gives to you. Therefore, you have to be willing to give in order to receive. In my personal experience, one of the ways that God trained me to give in order to receive is street evangelism. One of the things I loved and remember about street evangelist is that when I first began to witness to people, they would ask me all kinds of questions. At first, I had no clue as to what they were talking about when they asked me questions and I would get stumped because I was not consulting with the Holy Ghost but as I kept on evangelizing and as I learned to rely on the Holy Ghost, I was surprised at how the anointing would rise up within me to help me. After a while, there was not a question that someone would ask that the Holy Ghost would not help me answer. The Holy Ghost would not let the people confound me and the more I was willing to go out there and speak to the people, the more He would flow through me to help minister and answer questions.

Just like in evangelism, you do not have to worry about what will happen when you begin to speak into the lives of other people or fear that they are going to ask you questions that you cannot answer. When you are asked a question that you do not have the answer to, tell your mentee that you will get back to him or her another time with the answer. All you need is to learn to rely on the Lord and let His grace flow through you. Once you take a step of faith, the Lord meets you the rest of the way.

Receive Only the Truth and Reject Lies:

I discovered when I came to the Lord that apart from being our Savior and our Father, His next powerful role is that of a teacher. God loves having a good student in His classroom. The more you are willing to pour out to others that which He has placed within you, the more He will pour out on you. Therefore, you have to be willing to pass on to others the things that God has taught you in the scriptures and through your Christian experiences that line up with the Bible. Your experiences have to line up with the Word of God before you can pass them on to others, if they are not, please do not teach them to others. I will not share with others things that do not line up with God's Word. This is how I see myself: I see myself as a computer CPU in the Bible. Therefore, whatever anyone says to me has to line up with the Bible. When I hear something, my mind immediately references the Bible and does a search to confirm if what I have just heard is according to the Word of God. If what I heard does not line up with the Word of God or if it violates scriptures, an alarm goes off within me and it says, "nope, nope, nope." And you see me rereading that scripture to myself and if what I heard was not what the Word of God said, I will reject it no matter the status or social position of the speaker.

You will be surprised at how many preachers will trump up a scripture and then begin to draw all kinds of wrong, strange and weird conclusions from the scripture. They will knowingly violate the spirit and intent of the scripture in their attempt to manipulate the scripture to say what they want. You have to know the Word of God in order for you not to be deceived these days. The Lord gave us the responsibility to take heed that we are not deceived. Therefore, you are not going to stand before the Lord and say somebody deceived me. You are to test every spirit that speaks to you to make sure that it is of God. I said all that to say, that you must be grounded in the Word of God and the ways of God only. As you are grounded (well taught) in the Word of God, you can then begin to teach others so that they too can be grounded. You must pass on to others what you have learned but make sure that what you learned is the truth according to God's Word.

Example of Wrong Teaching:

I recently went to a conference and a very well known national and international speaker stood up and told us that all dreams are from God and that all dreams are about you; including your nightmares. He said that your nightmares are aspects of things you are running from; things you are refusing to face or deal with in real life. He further said that every single person that you see in your dream represents you and your stages of development. He said that everything in a dream is about you. I was shocked but I went back the next day because a pastor friend of mine was hosting the conference and we went to support him. Do you know that when we came back the next day that we were not up to 20 people in the church? The guest speaker cleared out that church because of wrong teaching.

This was the same man that packs out large arenas and auditoriums. One of the reasons people did not come back the next day was because, most of us have had dreams and some of those dreams have been nightmares, some of them have been about other people and some of them have been God's prophetic messages for others and not ourselves. Therefore, for someone to say that all your dreams are about you and that all your nightmares are things you are refusing to face in real life was very presumptuous and prideful.

Most people can remember when God showed them something about their relatives or their friends and the dream was not about the people that had the dreams. Another reason is because, there are times that we have had a dream or a vision about someone and have gone to the person and shared what we saw or dreamed and the person knew that it was the Word of the Lord to them. Such dreams and visions are not about us because we were just God's prophetic messengers and the dream or vision had nothing to do with us. This is why you need to know the scriptures for yourself so that you are not led astray by strange doctrine. I remembered sitting there thinking, "So when Nebuchadnezzar was dreaming about that image with the head of gold, the breast and the arms of silver, the belly and thighs of brass, the legs of iron and the feet of part iron and part clay, it all was about Nebuchadnezzar?" Again, when Pharaoh had his dream about the cows and the corn, it had nothing to do with Egypt because it was all about Pharaoh?" Thank God for His Word that showed us through these dreams and other biblical dreams and their interpretations that all your dreams are not about you and that it is possible to dream about other people, places and things.

You have to be careful of the things people are saying out there because what I am now discovering is that just because people are nationally known, they are using it as a platform to begin to pontificate and to postulate their personal doctrines. In other words, they are preaching and saying things pompously and pridefully without any biblical basis. You have to check the things that you are hearing, check everything that someone is saying to you so that you learn good doctrine and so that you pass on good doctrine. This implies that you have to be willing to go and search out scriptures for yourself. You have to know the Word of God for yourself because if you do not, you will be deceived because we have some "slick willies" preachers out there. Also, **Philippians 4:9** exhorts us as follows:

> **"Those things, which ye have both learned, and received, and heard, and seen in me, do: and the God of peace shall be with you."**

What Paul is saying in this scripture is, *"I am a walking demonstration of the believer; I am talking the talk and I am walking the walk. Watch me as I follow Christ and learn some things from me because I have made up my mind to follow Him all the way. I am purposed to be a walking demonstration of what I see in Him and what He has taught me. Learn from me so that you can do the same."* As a result, Paul was able to pass on to others what he learned from the Lord because those watching him knew that he was for real.

Also, when you look at the Lord Jesus in **John Chapter 17**, you can see His heart as you study His prayer. He said to the Father, "All that You have given to Me, I have given to them." In order words, I have mentored them (the disciples). He mentored twelve and God used the twelve and those who were in turn mentored by the twelve to change the world. If the Lord had just come, paid the price and left without anyone to pass on the message, only very few people would have been saved. Without equipping people to spread the Word, salvation will not reach all those that need it.

Those twelve reached others and today, we are still reaching others with the Gospel because this is the principle on which Christianity is based. It is true that Christianity is a confession but your confession must line up with your walk. Let others see your good example so that they can learn from you.

Note: The materials in this book were first presented in actual classroom settings.

Question and Answer Session

Mary: So, does anybody have a question? What is a mentor from what you have read so far? How would you define a mentor?

Grace: A mentor is someone who imparts the attributes and characteristics that are resident within them into another individual for growth.

Mary: So, the goal is to ensure that the mentee is being conformed to the image of Christ, right? Everyone that has read the book thus far should now be able to define a mentor, right?

Mary: Do you think mentoring is necessary?

Grace: Yes, I think that people come to a place in their lives where they get stuck and they see that there is a depth that God wants to get out of them. As a result, He uses other people that have already come into that place to impart that into them and that helps to get the individuals out of the place of being stuck.

Mary: What is a mentee?

Ashley: A mentee is someone who has a hunger and a thirst for Christ; for a deeper relationship and they decide to mirror Christ by exhibiting His character. Therefore, a mentee is a person who desires to be taught, who has a teachable spirit and who is looking for someone to show them things that will help him or her mature in the things of God. A mentee is someone who desires to excel spiritually and who looks for someone that is able to impart spiritual gifts and knowledge into his or her life.

Mary: So, would you say that there is a need for mentees to be raised up in the body of Christ today?

Ashley: Most definitely. There are a lot of people who are coming up in the church and they are receiving a lot from the church but they also need special attention. They have questions that they want to ask and they can receive answers to those questions if they have a mentor.

Mary: Basically, what would you say are the dynamics in a mentoring relationship?

Ashley: The dynamics of a mentoring relationship include someone who enjoys giving of themselves, sharing and pouring out to others what he or she has received and learned from the Lord. The mentor will teach the mentee and the mentee is someone who again, has a teachable spirit and is looking to receive input as well as correction when needed. The mentee does not mind being corrected.

Mary: What do you think a mentor will expect from a mentee?

Julie: A mentor would expect the mentee to set a desired outcome or goal that the mentee would like to achieve in their relationship. Both the mentor and the mentee would have to agree on the goals. The mentor would expect the mentee to have a willingness to grow, to receive direction, to receive instruction and/or guidance. A mentor would also expect the mentee to be honest and to trust the mentor's ability to guide him or her. They must both have a willingness and serious commitment to the mentoring relationship.

Mary: Why does the mentor need to know that the mentee is willing to grow and why is growth necessary?

Gina: The real point of the mentoring relationship is for somebody to grow; it is to help a person grow. The mentor needs to know that the mentee is willing to grow because growth is about change and change is not always easy and for some people, it can seem at times to be difficult. The Lord wants us to grow and He stretches us in the areas that we need it. The mentor needs to know that the mentee is willing to make the changes that the Lord requires and to do what is necessary to be conformed to the image of Christ.

Mary: Is it OK then, when the mentor challenges the mentee positively in order to bring forth the mentee's best potential so that the mentee grows in his or her relationship with the Lord?

Note: *Challenging the mentee is not to be a judgmental attitude or cruel treatment but one that really sees the potential in the mentee and challenges that potential to come forth.*

So, is it good for the mentor to put that type of demand on the mentee?

Gina: I think it is not only good but I think it is necessary. Like I said before, change can be difficult so we need somebody to challenge us. I know that our heavenly Father is the first one to challenge us because He wants us to achieve the plans and purposes that He has for our lives. So, it is out of love that He challenges us so that we can become what He has for us to become. Therefore, our mentors should challenge us likewise.

Mary: What do you do when you have a mentee that is not willing to be challenged or grow? What do you do with such a person?

Gina: You give them what the Lord has for them by telling them what the Lord is sharing with you about them to help them grow. They have a choice to agree or not agree with what the Lord is saying. You have to let them make the choice, it is up to them.

Mary: So, if you find someone that is not willing to change and they want you to go on the same cycle with them, that is, run around the same mountain over and over again, the mentor has to come to a place where he or she can say, "this is not working." Is it OK for the mentor to do this?

Gina: Yes, it is. It is OK but pray for them in love. Pray for them to have a heart for the things of God and above all else, pray that their hearts will open up to the Lord so that they can become teachable and correctable.

Mary: Praise God. I asked that question because it is not everybody that you are going to be able to mentor. There are times that you get people that are not teachable and they like to play the victim. When they speak, they make everything that has happened in their lives someone else's fault. They have mastered the "tune of victimhood" and they love to sing the same song to you over and over again without really desiring a change.

One of the things you really have to avoid in a mentoring relationship is developing a codependency type relationship. This is the type of relationship where you lend your shoulder to someone to constantly weep over and the person is not willing to make any change in his or her life. Empathizing and sympathizing with someone in their time of need is good and to be encouraged but when someone uses his or her past as a justification not to move on in life, you have to make sure that the person does not bring your life to stagnation as well. Therefore, there are times to cut some people loose.

Mary: Do you think everyone needs to answer all of the questions that we asked in the beginning of this chapter before embarking on a mentoring relationship? Do you think that it is also necessary for the mentee to answer any additional questions that he or she might have concerning his or her need for mentoring?

Jack: Yes, I think it is very important that we put an answer to these questions. We have to answer for ourselves if we really need another person's help in order to progress in our relationship with the Lord because progression is important to the Lord. Therefore, we must ask ourselves, "What is involved in a mentoring relationship and what is it that I really need? What is the difference between mentoring and counseling?" We must define why we should go to another person for mentoring.

I see the mentor as being the teacher and the mentee as being the student. So, it is our duty even as mentors to teach those who come to us. There are those who wish to learn, wish to know, wish to be corrected and who are hungry for the Word. Sometimes, you have to pull them aside individually and just completely teach them all that you can. Jesus Christ did the same thing. He did the same thing with John, His beloved one who was always with Him.

Mary: Praise God. To put it in another way, I would say that it is better for you to count the cost before you get into a mentoring relationship. I think that this is a good way to say it because the Lord Jesus Himself said that if you are going to build a house, you should first sit down and figure out if you can afford it because tongues will wag against you if you are not able to finish the building. Also, if you are planning to go to war, you must first count the cost so that if you discover that you cannot afford to go to war, you can then make peace with your adversary. Therefore, our end result is to make sure that we are going to be successful in what we embark on concerning mentoring. Yes, it is necessary to count the cost by asking yourself the questions that are listed at the beginning of this chapter.

Mary: What is the first thing you do before requesting mentoring?

Tammy: The first thing is to know that the Lord called me for a purpose. For instance, He spoke to me that He was going to use me to reach certain individuals. I did not feel equipped or prepared so I gave it time and I prayed. I prayed and asked God to align me with the mentor that He has for me in His time and for the purpose that He intended. Over the years, I continued to pray and desired to know exactly what He wanted me to do and who I would learn best from. Just as Ashley said, being teachable, having a desire to learn and having a hunger to actually reach the individuals God has for me to reach, means that I needed to be mentored so that I can grow. I thought for three years that it would be someone I would meet immediately but it was not until I met you, Mary that I knew that it was time.

Mary: You see, in Tammy's case, being here for mentoring is an answer to a request that she made to the Lord for mentoring. She asked the Lord to place a mentor in her life because God said, "ask and it shall be given unto you." Therefore, she asked, she waited patiently and in due time, God ordered her steps to my class. So, Tammy what you are saying is that this is something that God has for you and that it is the Lord that has orchestrated this phase of your training?

Tammy: Absolutely, because I know that I was not prepared. When He told me that He was going to use me, I said who me? I just waited for Him to open the door and it has been ten years. It is within the last three years that I purposed for the individual He has to mentor me and every door closed. It was when I met you, Mary at the church that I knew that you were to be the one and it was like, "Thank you." It was an answer and in a God timely way.

Mary: I believe the saying that "repetition is the law of lasting impression." Therefore, I am going to call on Gina to tell us some of the basic points that she can remember about the things that we have discussed so far concerning mentoring. She will tell us what a mentor is and what the dynamics of a mentoring relationship are. She will also remind us of how a person needs to prepare him or herself for a mentoring relationship.

Gina: In addition to everything that has just been shared, a mentor is somebody that leads and guides us to accomplish what God has for our lives. God's plan and purpose is to help us conform to the image of Christ and He will use mentors to accomplish this. A mentor is someone that God uses to speak His plan and purpose into our lives and to build His character in us. It is a person that God brings into our lives to show us exactly the areas that He wants us to grow in and to help us identify how we need to grow in those areas in order to achieve what He has for us.

We need to be prayerful and seek what God has for us, what His will is and who He wants to use to mentor us. It is not about our desires and what we want. It is about God's will and what He wants for us. It is when we come into alignment with God that we will really grow. God can then produce in us the things that He desires for us. Mentoring begins by prayerfully finding the person God wants to use and when He brings us in contact with the person, we have to be willing to change and we have to be willing to allow that person to sow godly seeds into our lives. This means that we have to really hear what God is speaking to us through the person.

I agree that we have to set the ground rules between the mentor and mentee so that the mentoring relationship can be successful. The mentor needs to be sensitive to the person seeking to learn from him or her. Both the mentor and the mentee need the grace of God to accomplish the tasks involved in mentoring. Specific goals should be set to measure the success of the relationship.

Once the relationship is established, the mentee needs to ask the Lord to help him or her with development and to give him or her grace to make the necessary changes. He will help the mentee to lay down the things that he or she has been holding on to that are not of God. At different stages of your development, the Lord will bring up everything that is not of Him at the stage you are in so that you can deal with them and He will pour into you the things that He has for you. The Lord uses the mentor for a season to develop certain characteristics in the mentee. It takes willingness and patience and not everything God is working in us is done in one season but God is faithful to accomplish the work He begins.

Mentoring is for growth and as I stated before, God can effectively and faithfully accomplish the plans and purposes that He has for our lives so that we can go out and begin to sow spiritual blessings into other people. He wants us to become mentors to the people He sends us to and to help them develop so that they can receive the things that God has for them. Mentoring is about building the right character and becoming equipped in the things of the Lord and we are to do it in love because love never fails.

Mary: That was very good Gina. For those of you who are just reading this section of the book, you basically have the chapter summarized for you. You can see that from reading Chapter 1 alone, you already have an informed view point on mentoring so that if someone should walk up to you on the street or in the church and say, "I want you to be my life coach or I want you to be my mentor," you are not going to be immediately lost as to what you are to do with the person. You can say to yourself, "I can have a handle on this request because I know where to begin. I will begin by telling the person to pray and I too will pray. I will also ask the person to outline for me some of the reasons why he or she needs mentoring. I will then ask myself if I want to mentor the person if God gives me an OK.

Knowing and Keeping With God's Blueprint:

You have seen from reading this chapter that successful mentoring will bring you into alignment with the blue print that God described in **Genesis 1:26** and that it will also challenge you in areas that God wants you to be challenged so that you can grow spiritually. Never forget that God set out in **Genesis 1:26** to make man in His image and after His likeness (character). Therefore, you can look at yourself and say, "I know that I am being transformed by the Word of God and I know that I am being made to conform to the image of Christ." Mentoring helps to guide and nurture you as you try to live a life of holiness and integrity so that you do not feel that you are alone. Your mentor is there to help you.

God wants you to be faithful to Him because when you become faithful, God can then trust you with what He has for you to accomplish for Him. The Bible says that most men speak well of themselves, but a faithful servant who can find? (**Proverbs 20:6**). God is looking for men and women that He can trust to faithfully represent Him according to His Word, His ways, His character and His mercy and His compassion. This is why we all need to be conformed to the image of Christ.

Chapter 2

Selecting a Mentor/Mentee

I say that in most cases, it is the person that desires to be mentored that approaches the potential mentor in order to establish a mentoring relationship. This means that we must not be afraid or become timid about approaching the person we admire for a mentoring relationship. Mentoring is of God and should be treated by both the mentor and the mentee as a great privilege from the Lord.

The Need for Prayer:

Prayer is a very vital aspect of our Christian life. Therefore, whether you have been instructed by the Lord or somebody requested mentoring from you, you still need to seek the guidance of the Holy Spirit on how you are supposed to proceed concerning the relationship. This means that the would-be-mentor must make prayer an important aspect of his or her life.

As the Lord uses you, there are times the He might say to you, "See that guy over there? He is your project for the next three, six, eight months or one year. I want you to take him under your wings." When this happens, what God is saying is, "I want you to mentor the person." When you receive such instruction, you have to go and pray for how God wants you to handle the relationship. You need a blueprint of what God wants in the person before you approach the person in order to bring the person under your wings. Also, you have to be able to look at the person and say from your perspective as the mentor, "What is it that this person needs?" As you evaluate the person, try to access where he or she might need your help so that you can come up with a plan on how you can best help the person. This means that you have to be able to put on a piece of paper or make a mental note of the reasons why the person might need mentoring.

The would-be-mentee would also need to pray and get an OK before speaking to someone about mentoring. He or she needs to make sure that they get an OK from the Lord and that mentoring is something that He wants them to do in the season that they are in. This means that you have to get a confirmation from the Lord that His plan and purpose for you includes mentoring and you must be sure before you take the steps towards mentoring.

If you get an OK from the Lord, then the first thing you do is to approach the potential mentor and make your request known to him or her. Sometimes, the people needing you to mentor them might be many as was in my case in which several people formally approached me to mentor them. In order words, they formally put in their request to me for mentoring and I went to the Lord and I asked Him, "How am I going to mentor all these different people?" I thought the number of people needing mentoring was a bit much but I was reminded by the Lord that I cannot have a problem that He cannot solve. He said to me, "class." His instruction was for me to set up a mentoring class!

You need to be patient after you have made your request known. You cannot be hasty in trying to get your would-be-mentor to give you an answer. Therefore, after you have put in your request for mentoring to your would-be-mentor, you need to exercise patience and you must not harass or pressure them. This is very critical because when people come up to you and want you to mentor them, or you are instructing people on how to mentor, you need to stress the importance of patience on both the part of the mentor and mentee. Mentoring is not something you jump into without seeking God first. After you have prayed and you have approached the person and the person is seeking God concerning your request, you need to patiently wait for the answer. Let your mentor-to-be hear from the Lord concerning your request. This is assuming that you also have heard from the Lord that it is OK for you to begin a mentoring relationship. Everything you do must be in God's timing, plan and purpose. Let your would-be-mentor also have an opportunity to seek the Lord and also get an OK from the Lord that he or she is the one called to mentor you.

The potential mentee needs to pray for the potential mentor to hear clearly from the Lord. As I stated in the beginning of this book, I did not know to pray for my potential mentor because the person I requested to mentor me never got back to me. I did not pray and she did not pray about it either. When I spoke to her, she just laughed. I think that she did not really know what to do concerning mentoring. I believe that if I had prayed or if she had taken it up with the Lord, maybe there would have been an outcome to my request. You do not want that to happen to you but I thank God for those that He later used to mentor me. I encourage you to pray for your potential mentor to hear clearly from the Lord concerning your request. Again, I say to you, release everything to the Lord and do not try to work the process; do not make calls and harass the person but just be patient and let the Lord minister to the person.

Making Jesus the Foundation:

Hearing from God before beginning a mentoring relationship is very vital because it helps us to lay a godly foundation. The Apostle Paul said in **1 Corinthians 3: 10-11:**

55

"According to the grace of God which is given unto me, as a wise master builder, I have laid the foundation, and another buildeth thereon. <u>But let every man take heed how he buildeth thereupon. *11* For other foundation can no man lay than that is laid, which is Jesus Christ</u>."

So, if you are going to build anything, you have to do it with the Lord Jesus Christ as the chief cornerstone. You must make sure that the Lord Jesus is the foundation of everything that you are trying to build; even if it is a relationship. This is why you need to pray and patiently get instructions from Him before you enter into a mentoring relationship.

It is wise as the potential mentor to find out a little bit of background about your potential mentee from the Lord. Pray for the Lord to reveal to you areas where you can help your mentee grow spiritually and how the relationship can be beneficial to the two of you. Your goal at this stage is to lay a foundation for the mentoring relationship to be established according to the Lord's will because you do not want to do anything that God is not asking you to do. God knows your schedule and you might be wanting with good intention to start a mentoring relationship and God knows that you are going to travel in the next two months and you just don't know yet. Therefore, He might say "NO" to you mentoring for a season. You might not understand why He gives you a NO, but you have to heed His instructions. You must be willing to lay down your plan and follow the Lord's plan for you because you have to be in the Lord's will. We all have to be in the Lord's will at all times.

"YES" or "NO" Response:

At this point, the potential mentee must be prepared for a "YES" or "NO" response. In other words, be prepared for the person you approached for mentoring to say "YES' to your request but do not become bitter if the response is a "NO." If the person says to you, "I cannot mentor you at this time," you should not be devastated by the response when it is not a "YES." Therefore, you need to brace yourself for either a 'YES" or a "NO" response.

As the potential mentor, you also need to pay attention and hopefully you have prayerfully considered the request that has been put forth to you. Do not blow anyone off just because you do not like the way they look, the way they smell or because they do not belong in a particular race or class that you are in. Make sure that you have heard from the Lord before you respond to a request because there are people that God places in our paths and it is our job to help them in their Christian walk. We cannot blow them off no matter what. The way I think about it is this, I believe that everybody in the kingdom has been given a "harvest basket" by the Lord (this picture helps me) and in this basket are all the people or all the souls that God expects each of us in our lifetime to bring into the kingdom or minister to. Each person's basket contains all the lives that are supposed to be changed by their sheer encounter with us and all the people we are supposed to speak the Word of God to. Yes, in your basket are the people that God expects you to help Him raise up. Be careful therefore not to reject them.

How many of you read the *Final Quest by Rick Joiner*? In the *Final Quest*, he recalled his experience of being taken to heaven and there he met a very well known minister that was supposed to have helped raise up Rick Joiner but the minister never took him under his wing to help raise him up. The well known minister died after operating a very successful ministry but Rick Joyner was allowed to speak to this minister in heaven. The minister then realized in heaven that one of the people he was supposed to have helped raise up on earth was Rick Joiner and that he dropped the ball on that. While Rick Joiner was making his way to the Lord in heaven, the prominent minister who barely made it into heaven cut through the line to speak with Rick Joiner and he apologized for the way he had treated him on earth. The minister saw that he missed the opportunity to help God raise up one of His major warriors! Had he helped to raise up Rick Joyner, then he would have had a major fruit in his harvest basket but he dropped the ball because he could not see beyond Rick's physical appearance. We are to learn from such mistakes by not rejecting people because of our personal idiosyncrasies.

Be Available to God:

There are times that God wants to transfer an anointing to another person to enable them to do what we do. This was the case with Paul, Timothy and Titus. God used Paul to raise up Timothy and Titus as well as other people. Therefore, when Paul was gone, his ministry did not just end. There were others who carried on what they had been taught by Paul. That is why for me, when someone puts a request to me, unless the Lord tells me right then that the person is not from Him, I will tell the person that I will pray and get the mind of the Lord on the matter. I do this because the Lord told me that if I do not learn to take things to Him for clarification in prayer, I can easily become the biggest persecutor of His new move or His new ways. He said this to show me why the most mature Christians are sometimes the worst persecutors of the new move of the Holy Spirit when they do not understand the move or when it goes against their established ways. Therefore, when someone comes to you and makes a request or you see a new move of the Holy Spirit, you should not discount it or reject it because it does not fit into your established mode of operation or doctrine. If you lean to your own understanding and judge it as something that is not from God, you can become the biggest persecutor of a new move of God.

This is why the Bible says in **Proverbs 3:5**, "Trust in the LORD with all thine heart; and lean not unto thine own understanding." Therefore, whenever you see something or someone makes a request to you about things of the Lord, take it to the Lord in prayer so that you can get His response. It helps you to know how to reply; for instance, when the Lord says "no," you know it is not your "no." If He says "yes," you know He will back you up, but if you lean to your own understanding, you can miss the "divine appointments" that God had set up for you because are you by-passing the leading of the Holy Spirit. You must learn to seek the guidance of the Holy Spirit. Therefore, make sure that you pray about every single request that is made to you. If you say "NO" to somebody and you later realized that God wants you to mentor the person, humble yourself and say, "You know what, I told you "NO" when you asked me to mentor you but I think that God really wants me to help you so that you can accomplish His plans for you. He wants me to help raise you up through mentoring." Do not be proud to admit your mistakes. Humility and love never fail.

Having Time for Mentoring:

Also, be sure that you are able to take on the responsibility of mentoring and that you have the time to invest in mentoring another person. Some mentoring relationships can last for a long time and some may last for a short while. For example, some mentoring relationships can last a year, some can last six months, some can last three and some can last two weeks but you have to let the Lord set the agenda. You can be in Virginia and God places someone in your path and for some reason at that point, the person is really close to you and it is like bam, bam, bam as you are sowing spiritual seeds into the person. When you leave, both of you might even promise to call each other but the calls never materialize because what you did not realize is that you had already invested in the person all that the Lord had for you to sow into the person for that short period. Then when you struggle to connect and make the relationship go someplace that God did not intend for it to, it will eventually dawn on you that you were only sent to speak into that person's life at that "kairo's moment." This knowledge then helps you to let go of the person. The Lord Himself might even confirm to you that it is not that the person does not want to be friends with you but it is just that God has not called you into any further relationship with the person. Therefore, the grace of God for the relationship is not there and you have to move on.

How to Give a Response:

You should give a verbal or written response to every request that comes to you for mentoring. Even if your answer is "NO," give a response anyway. Again, I say to you, do not just let it slide and never respond to the requests for mentoring. If it turns out that the answer is a "NO," how you say the 'NO" is very vital because we are living today in a society where people are very emotionally fragile.

A lot of people are already feeling rejected, abandon and neglected. Therefore, if your response to a mentoring request is a "NO," make sure that you communicate that "NO" to the person in a way that they understand that you are not rejecting them and that you are not belittling them or despising them. Give them the true godly reason that you cannot mentor them in the season that you are in. For instance, if your schedule cannot permit it, let them know. If the Lord says that this is not the season for you to mentor people, let them know that. I have had pastors tell me that they are not in the season to mentor people that come to them for mentoring so what they do is refer the people needing mentoring to another pastor whom they know is mentoring.

These pastors who are not mentoring understand where they are in the present stage of their ministries. Therefore, they are not taking on additional responsibilities that the Lord has not called them to take on. The flip side is that there are some people that do not know how to say "NO" to people so they take on more than they can handle. They end up making a wreck of things because they cannot keep up with the responsibilities that they have assigned to themselves. They promise and cannot fulfill their promises because they have overcommitted themselves. So, mentoring is something that you do not want to over commit yourself to.

Setting Time to Respond to a Mentoring Request:

Set a time for you to meet with the person who placed the request to you so that you can give them a response. I am now going to talk about your very first meeting with your potential mentee. This is the first meeting after a request has been made and both parties have prayed and each have received a "YES" from the Lord that that the mentoring relationship is to go on. There are some things that you need to pay attention to at this initial meeting. First, you need to set up a meeting time.

During this initial meeting, you need to stress the importance of honesty. Let the person know who you really are and listen to them as they are talking to you about themselves so that you can find out some things about them. Do not leave room for assumptions. Again, pray that the

Lord will reveal to you areas that you can help the mentee spiritually and physically and how the relationship will benefit the two of you.

It is during this meeting that you let the mentee know emphatically about your "Yes" because this step is really committing to the relationship. Even if your answer is a "NO," try to meet with the person that requested mentoring and in a nice setting, explain to the person what is going on in your life that does not give you room to mentor a person right now. If God has you in a season that makes it impossible for you to be involved in a mentoring relationship, let the person know. If the Lord said "NO," let the person know in a nice way that you may not be the person the Lord wants to mentor him or her. You are the one to set the tone at this meeting since it is you that requested the meeting.

At this meeting, you need to find out background information from your mentee. Find out about his or her life experiences in order to get to know them better and while you are doing this, do not assume the role of a counselor unless you are a trained counselor. Help them to understand what mentoring is about because some people might come to you thinking that because they are in a relationship with you, that you are going to help launch their ministry. **You have to be very careful to make your potential mentee understand that mentoring is to equip a person and to help a person develop godly character so that the person is prepared for the ministry God has for him or her.**

It is also during this meeting that you actually ask your mentee, why he or she needs mentoring. This will help you, because if the mentee is going to expect things from you that are outside your ability or that are not part of what you are called to do for him or her, this will help you to locate why the mentee is coming to you. So, just ask the mentee, "Why do you need mentoring?" Also ask him or her, the areas that your mentoring skills or the gifts of God that are operating in your life can be helpful to him or her. Be bold to ask the mentee, "In what areas do you think that I can help you?" Ask the mentee about the areas in his or her life that he or she thinks are currently very strong and the areas he or she thinks are weak.

Be Honest with Your Mentee:

You do not want to give an impression that something will happen in a mentoring relationship that will not happen. That is why you need to let the mentee know what you have learned about mentoring and you need to lay the ground work of what mentoring is about or what mentoring is not. I have had some people come up to me saying, "The Lord has given me a ministry and I need to come to you for mentoring so that the ministry can take off." This in itself is not bad if the Lord has revealed to you that this is His plan and purpose for them at the season the mentee is in. Also, if the Lord shows you ways that you can launch the person's ministry while you are helping prepare the person and you have the means to do it, by all means go forth. I may say to them, I do not have the means to help a person launch their ministry at this time but I can help you to develop godly character and give you an opportunity to learn what ministry is about so that you are ready for when God wants your ministry to go forth.

Assessing Your Mentee:

As I told you in the last chapter, when you talk to someone that has a limited knowledge of the Word of God, it shows. By the time you spend thirty minutes with your mentee, you can tell if he or she is a baby Christian and you can basically access where the mentee is in his or her spiritual walk so that you can begin to map out the areas where you can help him or her. As I also stated in the last chapter, you cannot grow above the Word of God that is in you. It is the Word of God that is in you that will determine the extent to which you grow because God does not operate outside His Word. You have to be challenged to know the Word of God in order to live a victorious Christian Life. We are all required to live by the Word of God. This is why the Bible says that, **"Man shall not live by bread alone, but by every Word that proceeds out of the mouth of God"** (Matthew 4:4). Therefore, every Word that comes out of the mouth of God is to be your food. You need to find out how much of the Word of God your new mentee knows. In **3 John 1:2,** we are told to prosper even as our souls prosper.

> **"Beloved, I wish above all things that thou mayest prosper and be in health, even as thy soul prospereth."**

I say again that from the above scripture, we can clearly see that our physical prosperity is tied to the prosperity of our souls. Therefore, if your soul is not prospering in the Word of God because the Word of God is the only thing that will cause your soul to prosper, then do not look for physical prosperity to manifest in your life. This is why we must know the Word of God so that we can live by it in order to prosper both spiritually and physically.

When we do a TV program and we start receiving calls as a result of the TV show, we have people that call thinking that there is some kind of entitlement that is owed them. Some of these people are not working and neither are they looking for work. They do not have a car and they are not willing to do anything to get out of the position they are in. Some of them have been waiting on the result of a law suit for years and they are not disabled but yet, are not willing to apply themselves. One even went as far as telling me, "Why do I have to have a job, why can't God just send me a rich man? Why do I have to go through all these changes when God is rich?" I said to her, "Do you think a rich man prays for God to give him a non-ambitious 'go-no-where-woman?' Do you think that a rich man is looking for a woman who is going to drain him and not be a blessing to him?" Therefore, we must each ask ourselves, "What do I bring to the table of marriage? What do I have to offer another person that will be a blessing to the person?" We must not be free-loaders and think that it is OK. We have to prosper in God's Word so that we can have success in every area of our lives.

When you look at your mentee or someone requesting mentoring from you, do you see an opportunity to check out their Christian walk? How is the mentee's walk lining up with the Word of God? Does he or she seem to you to be someone that talks the talk and walks the walk? You need to know this because there are people out there who know how to quote the scriptures in order to get people to listen so that they can get what they want. They might be doing it as a result of a flaw in their character or to get money or other things from other people. There are some people that just go from one church to another singing the same song until they get somebody that they think is gullible that they can hang around. Such people will use any reason or means including mentoring to get you to be their friend and if when they ask you for something you do not give it to them, you become a bad person and they move on to the next potential victim. You need to be discerning in weeding out these types of people from your mentoring program. Therefore, at this initial meeting, you need to see the seriousness of the person concerning mentoring because you cannot be anybody's God; only God is God. You have to be discerning.

Recommend Some Reading Materials:

Again, try to identify areas you are confident you can help the mentee based on the gifts of God upon your life. If you are not able to identify these areas, then pray for the Lord to reveal to you areas you can help the mentee based on what He has called you to do or how He has been using you. Basically, this meeting is for you and your mentee to get to know each other. During this particular meeting also feel free to suggest to your mentee to read a book on mentoring. This means that you have to have read some books on mentoring so that you can find out which books are good. It does not have to be a college program book but at least have a book you can suggest to your mentee to read so that he or she may learn something about mentoring.

Always remember that the goal of this initial meeting is for you and your mentee to get to know each other and for you to assess your mentee because sometimes you can think you heard from the Lord and you later discover that you really did not. Our personal desires might be so loud that we sometimes think that they are the voice of God but as you meet with your mentee or your mentor, you can get a confirmation from the Lord or you can tell when the devil is sending one of his agents your way. This meeting can help you to see potential "trouble" walking towards you and if you had leaned to your own understanding in thinking that God was the one sending the mentee to you. This is why it is very good to be able to ask questions that will give you an insight into the mentee's character and nature.

The initial meeting is an opportunity for you to speak to the mentee so that you can watch his or her response in order for you to see what kind of a person he or she really is. For instance, is the mentee a walking victim about things that have happened in his or her life? Is he or she a "codependence" just waiting to happen? Is the mentee emotionally stable? You need to know about these things before you get too involved in the relationship. If while talking to the mentee you discover that your answer of "YES" to the request for mentoring was a self-will "YES," then you should go to the Lord. Be honest and confess to the Lord that you had committed to a mentoring relationship that He had not ordained for you and that He should help you. He can deliver you out of the relationship or He might just give you grace to complete your commitment. The flip side is that you cannot use your dislike to rid yourself of people that do not appeal to you. Be a person of integrity and do not offend the mentee. Instead, after you have sought the Lord, you can have a gentle next meeting with the mentee and then say to him or her, "You know what, I do not believe that the Lord wants me to mentor you right now or maybe the Lord is calling me to mentor you, but I do not believe that the season is quite right." If the mentee needs to receive other professional help before they are ready for mentoring, let him or her know in a loving and kind way.

As I stated before, never reject the person or make the person feel rejected because some people get offended at members of a church and they fall away from God altogether. They might go like, "Oh those people, I don't go to church because they say that they are Christians but they don't act like Christians." So, do not be a vessel that runs people off from the Lord. I said that mentoring is like cleaning up the fish. After we have caught the fish or somebody else has caught the fish, somebody has got to clean them up. This is really where mentoring comes in. Mentoring basically takes a person and in a loving gentle environment tries to help the person develop godly character and values, unless of course, you determine that the person is not willing to grow. As I stated before, if you find that you are dealing with someone who is just looking to cry his or her victim-hood on your shoulder, you have to graciously bow out if they refuse to change as the relationship progresses.

Do not Ignore Warning Signals:
As I stated before, do not ignore the warning signs of emotional pitfalls such as emotional instability, codependency and other things that might show you that this person has some baggages attached to him or her that might distract you from the call of God upon your life if you are not very discerning. This is why I said earlier that some people can be an assignment to take up all your time. You can immediately see that the person is not going anywhere and he or she will see to it that you are not going anywhere also. When your phone rings, it is the person. You come home but you don't have quiet time anymore because this person knows your schedule.

There have been times that people put requests to me and the Lord would show me a vision:

This vision is usually about a mother with a crippled or paralyzed sick child sitting on her lap. The more the mother wipes the nose of the sick child, the more mucus comes out. The mother cannot get up and go anywhere or do anything because she has to attend constantly to this crippled sick child that is sitting on her lap and she has this endless job of wiping mucus away.

The Lord usually warns me with this type of vision so that I do not get into a codependence relationship that is not going anywhere. I always receive it as, "Don't get into that because they are sent by the enemy." It is true the devil will send someone to you to use up your time so that you do not have time for anything else. When you get yourself into this type of relationship, you are constantly being pulled on by the person. When you come home from work, the person will call you crying or there is already a message on your voice mail asking you to call him or her back.

This person is on your phone when you wake up and when you go to bed talking about the same thing every day. Do not make yourself a mother of a spiritually crippled child that is an assignment of the devil against your time and energy. One of the things I am very grateful to the Lord for is that He helps me to discern when someone is an assignment against me. Therefore, I am bold to tell the person, "Did we talk about this over and over before or for several times now? I am not willing to go around that mountain again with you if you are not willing to make the necessary change or take the necessary action." Do not get me wrong, I sympathize and I empathize with people when they need it or when they are in a crisis but I am not willing to do codependency with them. Codependency does not help the mentor or the mentee. It is just a time and energy killer.

Note: *These materials were first presented in actual classroom settings.*

Question and Answer Session

Cindy: You just touched on something from last year. I had a situation with a gal and exactly what you just described happened. There was a time that I was supposed to be there and I overstayed and it became codependent. I saw it and I did not know how to get out of it. Well, God got me out but I was hurt by it and I didn't see that my physical and emotional pains were the results of my allowing codependency. At first, I was just helping in the natural but when it became codependent, I was like how do I step out of this? God brought me out but it was very painful.

Mary: That's one of the major pitfalls of mentoring. How do you avoid codependence? If you work yourself into a state of codependence, you put yourself in a "catch-twenty-two" position. You will have difficulty getting out of it because you feel that you are bound to be there for the person and you will feel like a bad person if you let the person go. Also, you begin to think that God will be angry with you for not being there for the person, so you stay stuck in that relationship. This is why you must always go to the Lord in all that you do. I love running to the Lord about everything. I go to the Lord and confess that I messed up and I took this person on without His counsel or OK. It is a self work and I need His help to get out of it.

Julie: This question is about a person who insists on entertaining a victim mentality or tries to go back to situations that you have discussed before. Would you be kind to draw the line with them at the point of codependency? Would you put the relationship on hold and maybe tell them that when they feel that they are past the issue that maybe you two could resume the relationship or would you just terminate the relationship completely?

Mary: That is a very valid question and the answer to it would be very, very subjective. This is because difference people have different endurance levels. Some people might be more tolerant than others. For instance, Ashley might come to me from time to time because I am mentoring her. She might even call me one evening and as we talk, I realize that she has a problem and she asks me about it and I give her an answer. Let us say that someone has the same type of problem in class and the person raises the same type of question in class and we answer the question. Now, if the answer to the question was a solution that requires action on the part of Ashley, then I would be expecting her to take the necessary action. I will also be expecting the other person to take the necessary action as well. If the person in class took the necessary action and the problem is resolved for them and Ashley just wants to call me every evening now to talk about the same problem, I will not be a willing participant. Some other person might be willing to talk about the same issue everyday but not me. I will tell her to take action and stop talking to me about it.

This is why when you first meet people, you have to watch out for the codependent traits in them that might serve as a clue to you to be careful. Your spiritual antennas need to be up at your very first meeting with your mentee. This is why I also counsel you not to ignore the codependency traits that you see in a person. You can easily discern codependency because people that are codependent will talk and talk about the same thing.

An Example of a Codependent Trait

A few months ago, Gina and I went to dinner with some friends and there were some new people that had joined us. We were all getting to know one another and when we got to this one person, everything just stopped at the table as this person just went on and on about his victim-hood. This person talked about how life has been hell for him because of some job screening process that he went through. It was as though his life had stopped because of the incident. Finally, I asked him how long ago this was and he said four years ago! I asked him how long he had worked for the company and he said that he was not hired and never worked at the company.

You see, as he went on and on, I thought that it was something that had just recently happened and that was why he was having difficulty coping with not being hired but to my surprise, it was something that happened four years ago. Gina and I looked at each other because we knew the traits that we were seeing in this person. I also knew that we were witnessing a person who has been telling the same story for years and has really perfected how to tell the story in order to get the most sympathy. He knew when to punctuate the story for maximum effect for the feedbacks that he desired but Gina and I knew that he was a codependency just waiting to happen.

This is why I say that you have to be careful to listen when people are talking to you and that in mentoring, you have to be discerning so that you do not get yourself into a codependence situation. I knew not to volunteer myself as a sounding board for this person in the future. It is easy to tell when someone is a codependence victim.

To answer the question, I will listen to the person and seek the Lord for the person if there is a genuine need. The Lord is very on point with solutions and I will tell the person what I believe the Lord is saying that he or she should do or how he or she should handle the situation. But for those who are codependent, when they come around again and you ask them if they had implemented the solution, they will give you a reason as to why they have not. If you remind them again why they need to do it, they may give you another reason why they cannot do it. They will come around you again and again still talking about the same subject while they are still making excuses. As for me, I tell them that we have a saying in Africa that, "you can lead a horse to the river but you cannot force the horse to drink the water." I will cut the person loose when the person has exhausted my patience.

I will do exactly what the Lord does with me when He tells me to do something and I am trying to get Him to change His mind on the matter. He says, "OK, I will be waiting and when you are ready, just let me know." As far as the Lord is concerned, we are not qualified for any further instruction when we are in disobedience of the instruction that He has already given us. This is why the Lord will shut up from talking to us and we do not hear Him anymore concerning the situation that we are dealing with because He knows that we heard Him and that we are in disobedience. One time, I went to the Lord and He told me to do something and I wanted to pull one on Him so I told Him that I did not really understand what I was supposed to do. He said, you and I know very well that you understand; you understand very well so don't even go there. He was not going to deal with me until I did what He wanted me to do.

So, based on how the Lord deals with me, when I meet with people with a codependent or rebellious attitude, I do to them in love what the Lord also does to me in love. I am not going to be running around the same mountain with someone hearing the same stories over and over again. Some people will tell you that I have said to them, "I do not do codependency very well so do not go there with me." The bottom line is to give to people what God has given you for them that will enable them but if they are not willing to be enabled, then, they are not willing to be on the same page with you. You have to let them go.

Another Example of a Codependent Trait

Some time ago, I belong to an intercessory group and we usually had intercessory prayers every week and I remember one time that we had a prayer meeting and a young woman came to the group in tears and wanted the group to pray for her. She was pregnant and was in a very difficult place. She shared about her living and employment situations. Everyone was so moved by her story and we prayed for her. Two weeks later, she came up again and the group again prayed for her and people began to give her money and to offer different forms of help to her. Every week she would come up and we will pray over her and she would weep and some people would weep with her. Our weekly prayer meetings quickly became prayer time for this woman and she got a job after some months and she moved into a new apartment and the group was very happy for her.

Then, one day, someone came up to me and said, "I know that you all are trying to help so, so and so but she has been through three other churches with her situation." The person knew the woman very well and she proceeded to tell me that although this woman claims to love Jesus, she was fooling around with a man that was not her husband and that the man is married to someone else. She was pregnant with his baby but he has told her that he is not willing to divorce his wife. I confronted her and she admitted that the report was true about the baby and the man. I asked her if the man was supporting her financially and she said no. I talked to her over and over again about the need to live righteously and to be holy before the Lord. I told her that she needed to place herself in a position where she can receive and walk in God's blessing and that God was not going to bless her mess.

Guess who moved into her new apartment not quite two weeks after she got the apartment? That man that was another person's husband! I again confronted her when I found out that she had moved the man into her new apartment but she was not willing to do anything about him. She was willing to financially support this man with money from her new job so that he would not go back to his wife. One day, he beat her up and she came to the prayer group crying as she was relaying what had happened with him and I said to her, "Excuse me, this prayer meeting is about God, it is not about you. We cannot be coming here every week to pray for you while you are not willing to change. You use up all our prayer time every time we come together and by doing this, you are usurping the position of God in this meeting because we are stopping everything to minister to you but you are not willing to live according to God's Word." I said, "I am sorry, we are not going through that mountain with you again." After a while, she left and went to another group to cry the same story over there.

You have people that will always act like this woman but we have to hold them accountable in love. Does God not hold you accountable? You are not helping somebody by not holding them accountable.

Cindy: In mentoring, do you ever find that sometimes the mentees are toxic and when you are listening that you are not just listening with your ears but with all your being; mainly your heart and that you take in all the stuff? You find out that you take in all this information and you begin to feel what they feel through the heart of compassion and yet they are dumping all this stuff on you. How do you release it and get it out of you because their problems or their issues can sometimes become the mentor's issues?

Mary: I learned that very early on in ministry because the Lord Jesus taught me that He is the Savior of the world and not me and that He is my burden bearer. I do not let anybody make me their savior because God will abase anything that will exalt itself against His knowledge. When somebody starts to dump on me, I go to the Lord. The Lord will help you to release the burdens to Him and teach you how not to let people become toxic to you. He will also let you know when to cut them loose when they are not willing to change. I am at the point now in my walk with the Lord that the Lord shows me when a person is coming to dump on me. I used to minister to a lady who had converted from Christianity to Islam and I kept talking to her and talking to her and she kept telling me how she is using the Bible and the Koran and how she doesn't really have to be just a Christian or Muslim.

After a while, she began requesting that I pray Islamic prayers with her and she would try to remind me about Koran passages and verses that I had forever forsaken. I was being grieved by her and she was becoming toxic and when I sought the Lord about her, the Lord showed me a vision of her as a dog that does not want to be restrained and He told me to cut her loose. Therefore in my next conversation with her, I told her if she should die the way she was (abandoning her Christianity), that she would go straight to hell. I told her that God was listening to our conversation and that Jesus is the only way to God the Father. Therefore, she needs to make a choice for either Jesus or Mohammed. I cut her loose because I did not want her toxins.

Ashley: I know it's probably a good idea for women to mentor women and men to mentor men but are there times when it is OK for men to mentor women and women to mentor men?

Mary: Oh yes. The truth is that in Christianity, there is neither male nor female—this is our spiritual state but here on earth, there are still men and there are still women. A lot of men and women have fallen into sexual sin due to working in close proximity with the opposite sex. It has wrecked some homes, some churches, some organizations and tarnished many reputations. Former President Clinton is a good example of what can happen to a great man or a man of great influence when he mishandles a working relationship with a person of the opposite sex. It is just like the office secretary and the boss who are always working very closely together. There is a real danger in such close proximity with the opposite sex and in these days with the same sex (homosexuality) because you still have an active devil out there. This is why **Proverbs 6:32-33** says:

> **"But a man who commits adultery**
> **lacks judgment; whoever does so**
> **destroys himself. 33 <u>Blows and</u>**

**disgrace are his lot, and his shame
will never be wiped away**" (NIV).

The story of President Bill Clinton and Monica Lewinsky is forever written in the annals of history and Clinton will never be able to wipe away the shame and disgrace that it represents in his record and life history.

This is also one of the reasons why the Bible says to avoid the appearance of evil (**1 Thessalonians 5:22**). We are not just to stay away from evil but to avoid giving people the impression or opportunity to come to the conclusion that we are doing something that is evil. For instance, we have Ralph, Jack and others in this class but if I allow either Ralph or Jack to begin to hang around my house everyday in the name of mentoring (let's get real) it will give an appearance that something is going on between us even if there is nothing going on. Also, if I allow Daniel or another guy in the mentoring class to come to my house anytime he wants in the name of mentoring, you can be rest assured that it is just a question of time before the devil says, OK, how can I just sneak into this relationship and make it sexual, pervert it or just ruin it?

It is OK for a man to mentor a woman or for a woman to mentor a man but you have to use godly wisdom. You do not have to hang around with your mentee that is of the opposite sex in the name of mentoring. You do not have to conduct your meeting sessions in a fancy or romantic restaurant or in your homes. I will include male mentees in my mentoring program but I will do it in a classroom setting such as this. As you can see, this class is not all women but if I am meeting with a male mentee, you will find that another lady is there or it will be in a public place. For instance, I am not going to Ralph's house nor have Ralph sit down on my couch with his feet propped up and we are cuddled up together watching TV in the name of mentoring. That will not be appropriate and it is the reason why the Bible says to avoid the appearance of evil.

Do not be afraid to mentor the opposite sex. It can be done because the Bible says that you can do all things through Christ that strengthens you (**Phillipians 4:13**). You just have to make sure that you do not cross the boundary of what is appropriate because the Bible tells us to flee from fornication.

> "**Flee fornication.** **Every sin that a man doeth is without the body; but he that committeth fornication sinneth against his own body**" (1 Corinthians 6:18).

The Bible did not say that in order for you to avoid fornication, you need to bind the devil; neither did it say to cast him out. It says run! Idolatry and fornication are the two sins that the Bible tells us to flee from. God the Father told me that there is a reason He said flee fornication. He said, **"It is because I know what I have put in a woman."** There is something that God has put in a woman that can mess a man up no matter how spiritual the man is if he does not protected himself or if he lets his guard down concerning a woman. God made a woman to attract a man and there is something in a woman that a man desires and if the conditions are allowed to go unchecked, the devil can use that attraction to ruin a man. Also, women have to keep their guards up concerning the opposite sex. Always have someone else with you when you are meeting with your mentee that is of the opposite sex. You have to draw a line and pay attention to make sure that you do not cross the line of mentoring into ungodly fellowship. Ungodly fellowship can open the door for both the mentor and the mentee to be pulled down disgracefully.

Cindy: So, when you realize that something like this might be happening or is beginning to happen, because we know if an attraction is happening, do you just call it out and cut it off right there? How do you handle it because that's even in day to day life, you know?

Mary: The first thing you do for yourself is not to pretend that it is not there or that it is not happening. Call someone who has wisdom and counsel and confess to the person that you have been working with someone and you feel that the person is attracted to you or that you are attracted to the person and that you need wisdom. Tell the person the nature of the relationship so that the person can advise you to either cut off the relationship immediately or handle it differently. While you might be having a one-on-one mentoring session with the rest of the students, make sure that someone else is with the two of you whenever you are meeting with the mentee in question. Do not meet in private places with the person and cut off the relationship immediately if the attraction is very strong or is getting out of hand.

I got saved in 1992 and I have been in ministry for a while now but I do not go have drinks with a single guy in the name of preaching or ministering to the single guy. There are some guys that I have told to cut out their attractions to me because I know that they are not the person that God has for me. When you feed your attraction to someone or feed someone's attraction to you, you are setting yourself up for a fall if it is not the relationship God has for you. So, when you find that there is a pull on you towards a person or a person is being pulled towards you, call your brother or sister that you are confident will keep your business private to pray about it with you. Even if it is in the workplace and it is a job that pays you, there has to be a distance between you and the person while you pray. You cannot be praying and still be going out to dinner with the person.

There have been cases in which a lady would tell me that although she is already married, some guy told her that she was the one that God has for him even though he too is already married. Some guys would even go as far as saying that God told them that their current wife is not the real wife that He has for them and that the new lady that they just met or that they have been working with is really the one God has for them. I say to you, do not fall for such rubbish. Most of the people who fell for it have lived to regret it.

I have a personal policy and it is: I do not visit single men that I am ministering to and they do not come to visit me socially. If a single guy whom I am ministering to comes to me for any reason, I make sure Gina is around. I am not talking about dating here because it is different when you are dating someone. The person that you are dating will visit you and you will visit them. In this case, we are talking about professional conduct. When you are ministering as a single person, you need accountability because one of the things you have to be careful of is how you operate your ministry so that you are not accused of improper conduct. Always have someone who you can call on to hold you accountable. I tell my mentees that ministry is by reputation. You never want to subject your ministry to scandal or disgrace. Therefore, you need to be professional when you are ministering to someone or when you are mentoring someone of the opposite sex. Avoid situations that could lead to accusation of immorality or fornication in your ministry.

I love what Benny Hinn said about his early days in ministry. He said that he always made sure that his Administrative Assistant was an older lady. He was wise to recognize that as a single man in ministry, he did not need to find the most attractive Administrative Assistant that wears her trousers on the edge of her hips. Any man or woman who gets the most attractive opposite sex to work in close proximity with him or her is asking for it. Because, guess what, he or she will have plenty of opportunity to work very closely with the Administrative Assistant in the office area alone and the devil can make you fall at your moment of weekness. You must be careful because many men and women of God have fallen into sexual sins because of the opposite sex. Bishop Bill Hamon said during one of his sermons that the major pitfalls for men and woman to avoid in ministry are:

- The gold
- The gals/guys
- The glory (taking God's glory)

We all must avoid these pitfalls in ministry. He also outlined in his book titled, *Prophets Pitfalls and Principles: God's Prophetic People Today* the ten areas that ministers need to have in proper alignment in their lives in order to succeed in ministry. He calls them the "10 M'S" and these "M'S" have to do with your attitude towards ministry, money, motives, methods, morality, etc.

I have some people that say to me, "My joy is to go preach to homosexuals or to lesbians" and I would say to them, if you know that you have been a lesbian or a homosexual, do not go back to that circus saying I am ministering to them. The reason is because it is an area of weakness in your life and you have been delivered and need to stay delivered. Let those who are strong in that area minister in that area until the Lord raises you up so that you can minister in a classroom setting to people who struggle in that area.

I was watching a TV program a while ago and a prominent minister was on the program and he talked about how he now ministers to a large number of homosexuals in his church after his church split. The problem was that he was not requiring the homosexuals to make any lifestyle changes and he was affirming them in their condition! As I watched him, I realized that I was watching a man of God who has fallen and who no longer thinks that God's Word on homosexuality is the truth.

There was also another man on the program and he said that he started out as a youth leader or a youth pastor but got caught up in the homosexual lifestyle. According to him, he was determined to be rid of his homosexuality and there had been several attempts to deliver him from his homosexuality by deliverance ministers. Finally, he joined a ministry where he was prayed for and was placed in a house with two other men that were former homosexuals. They decided they were always going to be in the house praying, reading their Bibles and not go out on Friday or Saturday nights. They decided that they were going to be strong but do you know what happened in the group? The three of them began to engage in their homosexual activities right there in the house! This guy now believes that because people had prayed for him to be delivered and because he had gone through several deliverances and yet he and the other guys went back into the homosexual lifestyle, deliverance does not work. He is now convinced that God created him to be a homosexual. What he failed to realize is the power of association.

My question to whoever put three former homosexuals in the same house is, "What were you thinking?" He had set them up to fall back into their old ways by putting them together. Would you put three men that had been homosexuals in the same house? Their housing arrangement was a perfect setting for the devil to tempt them with their old vices. It is not true that the deliverance did not work but it was just the case of a dog returning to its vomit after being delivered. This is why you do not go back to where you know that you have a weakness after you have been delivered. It matters who you associate with.

Recognize your weaknesses and stay away from its temptation. Therefore, if you know that you once dabbled in some things and you got delivered, stay away from the things and their environment and do not deceive yourself by saying I am ministering to people that are bound in those areas. If you do it, I say to you that before you know it, you are going to be one of those people again. Do not submit yourself to the devil to be enticed in areas that you are weak. The devil will always try to use your former ways to tempt you but you do not have to fall or be in a place where you are constantly tempted. Although the Lord Jesus had no sin in His life, yet He was tempted according to the Bible, but He did not fall into the temptation.

> **"For we have not an high priest which cannot be touched with the feeling of our infirmities; <u>but was in all points tempted like as we are, yet without sin</u>"** (Hebrews 4: 15).

It is one thing to be tempted and it another thing to fall into temptation. It was sad that the man went away with the conclusion that God had created him to be a homosexual because he fell into the temptation of the homosexual lifestyle. What he did not realize is that it is possible to be tempted and not fall into the temptation. The Bible also tells us that "with God all things are possible" because there is nothing that God cannot do. Therefore, submit areas where you are weak to the Lord for His grace to help you.

Note: *This assignment is an example for those who will teach mentoring in a classroom setting.*

Class Assignment

This class is a little bit different because it is not a one-on-one session in which I can ask you questions privately as I had outlined them in the manual. Therefore, I have an assignment for you. I want you to outline for me, your reasons for needing a mentor. I will collect the answers at the next class and we will discuss them durring our individual one-on-one sessions.

Chapter 3

Starting a Mentoring Relationship

This chapter deals with starting a mentoring relationship. This is after you have had the initial meeting with your mentee and both of you have decided that you are going ahead with the mentoring relationship and you as the mentor have also had an opportunity to get an insight into your mentee. Hopefully, the mentee has also gained an insight about you as his or her mentor. When this happens, you are now officially starting a mentoring relationship. In this particular part of the relationship, the first thing you need to do is make sure that you define the nature of the relationship so that the two of you can have a good understanding of what this relationship is all about.

Having a Mutual Agreement:

This means that you and your mentee have to decide how the mentoring is to be carried out. Is it going to be mentoring over the phone? Is it going to be a one-on-one mentoring by visits? Is it going to be the type of mentoring where you meet at some restaurant or in your home or the mentee's home? In order words, what will be the nature of the interactions? How do you see yourselves working it out? Depending on what is going on in your home environment, it is not everybody you want to come to your home and you may not be able to go to all your mentees' homes. The reason for this is because there are some very good Christians whose spouses are very antichrist, so you can not go to their home for Christian activities. Therefore, you and your mentee must decide how and where your meetings will take place. If there is a problem in this area, then pray for the guidance of the Holy Ghost.

Having Good Time Management Skills:

I told you in Chapter 2 that **a mentor is defined as a wise counselor or teacher.** This means that the things that are deposited in you by the Holy Spirit need to be passed on to another. Mentoring gives you an opportunity to impart those things into the life of the mentee but you have to do it in meetings at the times agreed upon. I give you a key and it is found in **2 Timothy: 2:2**. The Apostle Paul is speaking to Timothy saying:

> **"And the things that thou hast heard of me among many witnesses, the same commit thou to faithful men, <u>who shall be able to teach others also</u>."**

It is great to impart the things that God has given you to another person but just because you are mentoring a person does not mean that the person always has to use up all your time in the name of mentoring. Learn to use your time wisely. You and your mentee have to develop an action plan that involves good time management skills. In this action plan, you are going to decide how frequently you will make contact with each other. You are also going to decide the duration of each meeting. What you are trying to do is set boundaries. If you say that you are going to meet with somebody for one hour, two hours or three hours, keep to the time. Do not violate another person's time and do not allow somebody else to violate your time because if you are married, you might give occasion to your spouse to be angry because of too much time spent away from home. So many women whose husbands are not in the church or are not strong in the Lord do not use wisdom when it comes to the things of God or their church activities. By their actions, they pit the Lord Jesus against their husbands. In other words, the time that they spend away from their spouse becomes a contest in which the Lord is their spouses' rival for their time and affection. Some men are also guilty of this too. Their spouses' major complain is that they are always in church and if you have an opportunity to speak to their spouse, he or she might say to you, "I don't see my wife or husband anymore because he/she is always in church and if it is not church, it is some church related something."

Therefore, you have to use wisdom in dividing your time so that you do not make the church or the Lord Jesus a rival or a competitor with your spouse. You need to set boundaries for your mentee so that when you step into a meeting with him or her, you know exactly how long the meeting is going to last and you need to keep to the duration. You do not have to be legalistic about it but basically have some parameters as to the duration of each meeting. For instance, do not come together with your mentee for a quick thirty minutes meeting and it turns into an all day thing. If you keep that up, you will have to always explain to your spouse why you were away all day. If this continues week after week or month after month, you will have a fight on your hands with your spouse. Do not allow mentoring to destroy your home.

Determining if Mentee is Spirit-filled:

In your second meeting with the mentee, you need to find out from your mentee if he or she is Spirit-filled. If your mentee is not Spirit-filled then, you need to give him or her the Gospel of Jesus Christ and you need to help him or her to understand that we can not do anything in our own strength. Your first meeting with your mentee was to basically respond to the request for mentoring and to get to know the mentee as well as the mentee getting to know you. It was also to identify why the mentee needed your mentoring skills but in this second meeting (hopefully you and your mentee are in a place where you both have an insight as to what the mentee needs), you want to make sure that your mentee is filled with the Holy Spirit. Help your mentee to know that we need the power that God gives us from on High because Jesus told us in **John 15:5** that without Him, we "can do nothing." Then, pray with your mentee to become Spirit-filled.

Mentoring in the Workplace:

If you happen to be coaching (mentoring) someone in the workplace, it is not the time or place in many corporations here in the US for you to bring in the Gospel. Your goal therefore will be to help the person understand how that they "need the higher power" (just so they understand) to help guide them in order to be successful in life. If the person is not ready, then leave him or her alone. You have to be sensitive to the spiritual tone in your workplace so that you do not loose your job. You need to apply wisdom because the Bible tells us in **Ecclesiastes 7:12** that "wisdom is a defence." The following can only be done in a work environment if the person that you are coaching or your mentee is already a Christian or is receptive to the things of the Lord. If you know that the person is in need of salvation, try to meet with the person outside of the workplace so that you can give him or her, the Gospel of Jesus Christ.

Impartation Session with Your Mentee

If your mentee is willing and ready to be Spirit-filled, you can then pray with him or her to receive the baptism of the Holy Spirit. If he or she is already Spirit-filled, this particular meeting which is your second meeting is an opportunity for you to implement your initial impartation. You pray for your mentee by laying your hands on him or her and asking the

Lord to release through you the anointing that will help him or her to receive what God has placed in you for him or her. Release the gifts of the Spirit upon your mentee as your hands are still on his or her head. There is a grace that your mentee needs in order to be mentored by you. It is critical that your mentee receives from you an impartation of the grace of God that is upon your life.

Even during this session, you are still trying to get more and more insight about the character of your mentee. Hopefully, the mentee is also trying to find out more information about you in order for him or her to understand you better because the goal is for you and your mentee to grow in this relationship. For example, if you work with me a while, you know that when Mary says, "Let's do this" or when we have agreed that something is to be done, we are going to do it. Therefore, if when we get back together the thing is not done, I'm going to ask, "OK, what happened?" If the reason is understandable why it was not done, I am fine because there are some circumstances that we cannot help or avoid but if I notice that it is a pattern, I will have a talk with the person. I will tell the person that I do not appreciate someone coming in to waste my time neither do I want to waste anyone else's time. I want to use my time wisely and will not let anyone waste it.

Avoiding Emotional Baggages:

You do not want to be the constant recipient of someone's emotional baggage. The question that Cindy asked in the previous chapter was, "What do you do when people are trying to dump emotional baggage on you?" I said to take it to the Lord in prayer before you do anything. The Lord is the Savior of the world and He alone died for us all and apart from Him we can do nothing. If you get an OK from the Lord to let the person go, then by all means, cut the person loose. There are some people that you will have to tell in a nice way, "I did not die for you but Jesus did so let's seek Him." This is one way that you can help someone that is codependent on you and is dumping all their emotional baggage on you. Try not to give codependent people your own opinion but seek the Lord and give them the Word of the Lord that you received for them. This way, you can always keep a person from dumping all the baggage on you and making you feel responsible in a way that God has not called you to. He warned me in the beginning of my ministry. He said to me, "Do not lead people to yourself; you have to lead people to Me."

The reason is because, some years ago, I had this one long prayer on a legal size paper (**The Cleansing Prayers** and **Prayer to Rebuke Evil Spirits** in Volume 1 of my **Effective Prayer** books) and the prayer was a big hit. I gave it to a few friends and it quickly spread because people were just giving it to their relatives and they were praying the prayer. One day, I had an opportunity to meet with some of these people and their relatives, and they were all going Mary this and Mary that. Everything about the prayer was about how wonderful Mary was and what Mary had done for them with the prayer. It got to the point that it began to bother me that they were calling my name instead of the Lord's name. They were saying what my prayer had done instead of what the Lord did with the prayer. They never mentioned the Lord Jesus.

Therefore, when I left them I said Lord, "I don't want to take Your GLORY. What is going on with this picture? Something is wrong with it" and He said to me, "You are leading them to you and not to Me. Therefore, they are out there singing your praises." I was like oh, this is bad. He then told me to lead people to Him and not to myself. He is the one that died for them and He is the Savoir of the world and not me. Since then, I have learned not to lead people to me but to lead them to the Lord. I do not want people singing how great I am but I want them to sing how great the Lord is. After all, nothing happens if He does not answer the prayers!

I have to keep this in front of me all the time, especially in mentoring relationships. I think that we all have to know that it is not about us but about the Lord. Knowing this will help us to release burdens and people to Him and it will also keep the people from dumping their emotional baggages on us. Again, I say that it is the best solution for eliminating codependency. Unfortunately, there are some people that even your best efforts will not be able to help in deflecting their codependency habits and traits and you have to know when to cut them off.

Let the Word of God be Your Final Solution:

Make the Word of God your final solution with your mentee. This means that when things get rough, the Word of God is the last word that you give to your mentee because if you give your own words, he or she might wrestle with you or argue with you with a counter opinion. If it is the Word of the Lord that you gave them, you can always tell them, "You will have to pray or let the Lord explain that to you because I didn't write the Bible." If they want to wrestle, then let them go wrestle with the Lord and His Word. We know who always wins. God will not change His word for anyone of us no matter how much He loves us. This does not mean that you have to use the Word of God to manipulate your mentee or your mentor.

The Word of God is sharper than any two edged sword and when you are speaking the Word, it is speaking you. When you are reading the Word, the Word is reading you also. When a person comes to me and gives me all the excuses as to why they cannot do something, I tell the person that I understand but according to the Word, they cannot get what they are asking for without obeying God's Word. Therefore, be quick to give people the Word of the Lord but avoid quoting the Bible at them or beating them down with it. I am talking about keeping the spirit of the Bible as it is written:

> **"...For the letter killeth, but the spirit giveth life"** (2 Corinthians 3:6).

We must never use the Word to manipulate or coerce people to do what we want them to do. Always remember that God gives us all a free choice. Therefore, a person has a right to choose whether they want to obey the Word of God, your godly counsel or a "spiritual principle." Never take that away from your mentee. For instance, if I have somebody who does not know the Word of God and the person has several excuses as to why he or she does not know scriptures and does not have time to study the Bible at home or go to a Bible study or church, I will just give him or her the scripture in **3 John 1:2**:

> **"Beloved, I wish above all things that thou mayest prosper and be in health, even as thy soul prospereth."**

I will tell the mentee to examine the above scripture very well if he or she desires to see physical prosperity. As I stated before, according to this scripture above, if your soul is not prospering spiritually, do not look for prosperity in the physical.

The mentee will not be able to say that Prophetess Mary said that I am not going to prosper because I am not reading the Bible. I am not the one who said it but the Word of the

Lord. So, if the mentee wants to wrestle with the Word, let him or her go wrestle with the Lord. I do not think that you and I are ever going to find somebody that God is going to give a huge pat on his or her back and say, "Well done good and faithful servant, you can't get into My Word, you can't pray because you just have too many things going on in your life and therefore, you have no time for Me; bless your little heart." Not one person will get that from the Lord because the Bible tells us to **"seek ye first the kingdom of God, all these things shall be added unto you"** (Matthew 6:33). When you place God first in your life, He will make things work together for good for you. Therefore, learn very quickly to put God first, to lead people to Him and to point them to His Word for answers.

Defining Your Mentee's Life Purpose:

Help your mentee to determine the thing that defines his or her life purpose. Everyone of us has a life purpose and we can grow in it, we can improve upon it but it does not change. For example, for me, integrity, truth and wisdom are very strong in my life purpose. Integrity is such a key foundational element with me that when I meet a person and there is lack of integrity in the person, I cannot relate very well with the person because I do not see a foundation to build anything on with the person. I might be hugging, laughing and talking with the person, but I would still make up my mind that the person is a "no go area" because there is no integrity.

When someone tells me something and it does not check out, I put the person in a "no go category," just like you have a basket or shelve where you place things that you are not using. The person can give me a million dollars tomorrow and I will say, "Thank you" but the person is still in that "no go" basket or shelve. Now, some people's life defining purpose might be totally different and as a result, integrity, truth and wisdom might be secondary to them. Therefore, they can listen to excuses for a long time before they get fed up with the person and then make a decision to let the person go. This does not mean that we all do not operate at a level of desiring integrity or desireing to support others, but the intensity or primary requirement differs from one person to another. You have to find out, what is the one thing that you look for in a person when you first meet the person? What is it that a person does in your encounter with the person that makes you decide right then if the person is good to associate with or not?

You have to know what the thing is that motivates you and helps you make critical decisions in life. It is something that God placed in you and you will find that from the time you are little, it has really played a vital role in helping you to determine who you will allow in your life and who you would not. Therefore, when you are meeting with your mentee or you are meeting with your mentor, try to see what it is about him or her that shows their life purpose.

<u>Note</u>: This assignment is an example for those who will teach mentoring in a classroom setting.

Class Assignment/Activation

Mary: What we are going to do in this particular session is have our impartation but before then, I want you to hand in your assignment from the last class. <u>I gave you all an assignment last month asking you to outline for me, your reasons for needing a mentor</u>. So, turn in your answer to the question. I also need you to tell me the book(s) that you have read so far on mentoring. I suggest the book titled:

Guardians of the Gate: Enriching Your Life Through Spiritual Mentoring by Ann Platz.

How many of you have read Watchman Nee's *Spiritual Authority?* It is a good book and I highly recommend it.

Today, I have another assignment, because this is going to help me with your one-on-one meeting with me. The question is, <u>what are the areas that you think that I can help you as your mentor</u>? This is addressing the areas that you think that I can help you as I mentor you.

The next thing that I am going to do now is move into an activation session because I want to lay hands on you all so that you can receive the anointing to be mentored and to mentor other people. You all need this anointing because when you finish this training, you will know what to do with another person as far as mentoring is concerned. Does anyone have a question in this area?

<u>Note</u>: Remember that these materials were first presented in actual classroom settings.

Question and Answer Session

Julie: I have a question about the agendas being set in a mentoring relationship. Do the both of you set the agenda from the beginning? Does the mentor deviate at anytime? I ask this question because, I was thinking, what if it is something that the mentee has problems with? Do I throw the baby out with the bathwater?

Mary: I don't think agenda is the word, I think it is called action plan. You need an action plan for anything that you do. You have to have a vision because without a vision, you and your mentee are going to go around in a circle and without a vision you cannot really tell if you are being effective in the life of the mentee. For instance, if you come to me and say, "Mary, I want to be groomed for ministry and these are the areas ... that I see you operating in that I think are going to benefit me. Therefore, I need for you to help challenge me in these areas because these are the areas that I struggle in." Now, I am not going to remake your identity or who you are physically. I am only going to help you develop in the areas that you outlined and that you and I have agreed upon assuming that you are really serious about being challenged in those areas. Nothing is set in stone that cannot be changed by the mentee or the mentor in an agreement because we are all still growing in Christ; but for the season that we are in a mentoring relationship, we have a set goal.

The objective is to achieve this goal in the life of the mentee but if the mentee turns out not be serious or committed to achieving the goal, then, the mentor must address the situation. Worst still, if the mentee is lacking in integrity and is of a dubious character and is not willing to change, there might come a time that the mentor will have to let the mentee go. I do not regard this as throwing away the baby with the bath water but more like knowing when to stop going around the mountain with someone who is really not willing to change. So, you see that this is more like goal setting instead of agenda setting because agenda setting can be totally within the control of the mentor but when the mentor and the mentee come together and agree on a goal, they should both try to accomplish the goal. For example, I told you to write down on a paper for me the reasons why you need mentoring. These reasons should be valid for the level of your Christian walk right now.

Now, after I have mentored you in this season, you might have other reasons for needing further mentoring in other areas down the road. The reason is because in Christianity, God expect us to grow constantly. For instance, in a couple of years, you might need further mentoring because you are now at another level in your Christian growth. Also, when you begin the ministry that God has for you, your mentoring needs may differ from before you entered into ministry because you are now out there and there are things that you are going to encounter in ministry that will challenge your faith as a Christian. When people out there challenge your faith and ability to trust by their actions and their words, if you do not have somebody guiding you, you might get so angry that you start operating from a judgmental point of view. Believe me; you will be shocked by the ways that some people and some churches treat you. Therefore, you are likely to need mentoring at different stages in your ministry. Nothing is ever set on a stone in Christianity except the Word of God—the only truth there is!

I say to you again that you do not throw away the baby with the bath water but remember to take everything to the Lord in prayer. Let the Lord be the one who decides what you should do when you are being challenged by your mentee or your mentor. As a mentor, there might be some people that you insist on mentoring and God might be saying NO to you mentoring them. If you are not discerning and insist on mentoring them, you are going to have friction in your mentoring relationship with them and in the end when things do not work out, you will say to yourself, "I wish I had listened to the Lord and let them go." This is why you have to be discerning in order to make sure that you are not ruled by your own emotions but that you are led by the Holy Spirit. Our emotions and good intentions always have a way of getting us in trouble. For instance:

Once I picked up a young lady from the street because she had nine month old twins as well as a three year old child. As a new Christian, I had zeal without knowledge and I wanted to do all these things for the Lord so I moved her into my apartment. All the while she was with me she refused to make any changes in her life style. The last straw came when one day, I came home to find her smoking. When I tried to talk to her about it, she said to me, "You knew how I was before you let me come into your apartment. After all, Jesus said 'Come as you are.'" I told her that Jesus loved her too much to let her stay as she was and that I personally would not tolerate certain behavior while she was still living in my apartment and I walked away. She followed me and began to sound off on me about "me and my Christianity." She entered into the bathroom where I was and said some things to me and banged the door.

When I saw her desire to attack me, I turned on her just one time and she got scared because she discovered that I was not one to back down out of fear. I had to let her know who she was dealing with and she knew that she was dealing with someone who did not take nonsense. I had to let her see that there was a side of me that can effectively deal with her type and I said, "You are out of my apartment." Before this time, I had met with her mother and I demanded to know from her why she would throw out a daughter that has nine month old twins and a three year old.

She then informed me how she had taken the three year old girl when she was just a baby and wanted her daughter to make changes to her lifestyle but instead, she was back at the club and again came home pregnant with a set of twins.

According to her, after nine months of watching her go back to the same lifestyle, she decided that she had had enough. She had decided that she will no longer play nanny while her daughter was out there in the clubs. I went to the Lord in prayer concerning this lady and my decision to let her go and it was then that I learned from the Lord that I had gone into the situation without His permission or direction. I then told the Lord that I would never again do something like that without first consulting Him. I will never again operate out of good intention or with "zeal without knowledge."

Emotions are good because we are still on planet earth but when they conflict with being led by the Holy Spirit, I will take being led by the Holy Spirit over my emotions any day. A lot of people are in trouble in their Christian walk today because they are leaning too heavily on their understanding and their emotions. Sometime, I look at them in a conference or on a TV program and they are going, "ooohhh" while rolling or falling on the ground and the preacher may not even be preaching! The preacher might be saying the same thing over and over again and what he or she is saying might not be scripturally correct but still, these people are crying, shouting, falling down or rolling on the ground. They are all fired up in their emotions and at the end, they go home and nothing has changed in their physical circumstances. They cannot discern "Sleek Willy Preachers" in order to stay away from them because of their emotions. There is one scripture that I hold on to for dear life—**Romans 8:14**:

> **"For as many as are led by the Spirit of God, <u>they are the sons of God</u>."**

We have to always be led by the Holy Spirit so that we are always in God's will for us at all times. God alone is all-knowing and He knows when we are about to get in over our heads in a situation. So, I say again that there are some people that God might have you to let go and it does not mean throwing the baby away with the bath water. You just may not be the person called to mentor them. Therefore it is good to be led by the Holy Spirit. Here is another story about a guy that I met that was being led by his emotions.

> *This guy told me that he loved picking up hitchhikers because he believed that it was the ministry that God called him to. Therefore, he would go out there looking for hitchhikers and he would pick them up drive them to different places. He was so happy doing it that he would be singing glory, hallelujah until the Lord said to him, "If you get yourself killed, do not blame it on me because I did not send you to pick up hitchhikers." He said that he was shocked because he thought he was doing all these good deeds for God.*

It does not mean that God does not love the hitchhikers or that this guy loves hitchhikers more than God. What it means is that this guy was not called to pick them up as he was doing. He was actually endangering his life by picking up anyone that he sees on the road side. When God sends someone to pick up a hitchhiker, God will protect the person. For instance, if you are on the road and the Lord says, "Stop and pick up that person," the grace of God will protect you but if you take it upon yourself and call yourself the "roadside rescuer," you just might see Jesus before you are prepared. God is not obligated to protect us when we are doing self-willed acts or iniquities.

Also, when I was in New York and before I got saved, I decided that I wanted to make a difference in people's lives so I went and volunteered in a Suicide Prevention Hotline. I would go in on a Friday and they would lock me and the other people in overnight in a secret location. Once in, you are in for the night and you cannot come out until the next day and no one is allowed in until morning. I never thought about it but if there had ever been a fire while I was in there, it would have been the end for me and the people in there because none of us had the key! The manager only comes in the morning with the key. The way she looked at it was that she was protecting us from crank callers; some of whom are ready to take their own lives and can be serial killers.

I was glad to be making a difference in the lives of the many people who constantly called this hot line. Some were very intense in their desire to end their lives and some were easier to talk out of their decision. There were some that were just simply crazy and they would call every day but we were required to talk them out of their decision anyway. We had a script that was given to us to follow and it also had answers to some questions they might ask. Some of the callers knew the script and when they tell you how they are going to kill themselves, they knew what the script says to tell them but many of the callers truly wanted to end their lives. Therefore, I thought that I was doing a public good by making a difference in their lives.

I never really paid much attention to the reasons why I decided to volunteer for the work. I was not being paid for the job but I was glad to do it. I decided to volunteer for the job because my conscious was being pricked because I felt that I was in a good place financially and therefore was at the point that I should begin to give back by sowing into the lives of others. It was not that I was rich financially but I was doing well. I talked to a friend about volunteering at a community service program and she referred me to the Suicide Prevention Hotline Program.

Not long after, I became born again. When I moved to Georgia from New York, the spirit of suicide began to bombard me everywhere I went. It will tell me to kill myself and would even point out how I should do it. One thing that I know about myself is that I do not have a fluctuating personality of "depression vs. happiness." I do not get depressed; I do not have a good day and a bad day. If I have a problem, I deal with it and I am not suicidal but this spirit kept telling me to kill myself and I kept rebuking and telling it that I have no reason to want to kill myself.

Because I was new in the Lord, I did not take it to the Lord immediately but I eventually went to the Lord about it and I wanted to know why the devil was harassing me this way, He said, "Remember your good intention work?" I said, "What good intention work?" He said, "Your suicide prevention work. Remember when you were helping the people that were suicidal?" He said, "What exactly were you telling them? Did you ever tell anyone of them about Me? Did you even point them to Me?" I said, "No." Then, He told me that because I did not have the spiritual power from Him to deal with the spirit of suicide, what I was doing was actually having fellowship with the spirit because He alone gives the power to drive out the spirit.

Therefore, rather than me driving the spirit away, I picked it up from the people and the devil was trying to use it against me because he knows that I had picked it up from the people! He told me to repent of my iniquity and He would drive the spirit away. I repented and renounced the job. I also came out of the Suicide Prevention House spiritually and physically in prayer and I renounced every agreement that I had ignorantly made with the spirit through the people and I never heard from the suicide spirit again.

What happened to me represents what can happen to people that are led by their good intentions and their emotions. I woke up one day and said, "I'm going to help people that are suicidal" and I was not sent by the Lord. As good as it seemed, it was still an act of iniquity. Also, I went to the job without being equipped by the Lord for it. This is why you see some people that are not born again and are not Spirit-filled but are working in a facility where the patients are spiritually afflicted begin to exhibit or manifest the looks and the ways of their patients. Some of them begin to get vexed at night by the same spirits that are in their patients. It is one of the reasons that I advise people who work with mentally afflicted patients to lift their jobs to the Lord in prayer so that He can protect them from the evil spirits that are in the patients. You have to be led by the Spirit of the Lord in everything you do so that God can protect you.

Elaine: Mary, I have about eighty to a hundred students and about ten percent of them want mentorship but, I am in a work environment whereby they don't really celebrate Christianity. So, how do I bring in Jesus and have that spiritual principle you were talking about?

Mary: Remember that I said previously that mentoring is called "coaching" in the workplace? The principles of the Lord are the same whether you attach His name to it in the workplace or not. If you look at the people who are successful today, you will see that many of them are using biblical principles. A lot of the successful "unbelievers" around today are recipients of the benefits of a godly foundation or a godly principle that one or more of their ancestors had tapped into but because they are using their riches and influence to live for themselves, they do not know to give God glory for it. You can apply godly principles in your life, in the church and in the workplace. For instance, honesty is honesty inside and outside of the church. Getting to know who you are going into a relationship with or being discerning about who they really are, is the same everywhere. This is why you can take these mentoring materials and present them in any place. You can hold the same class in the workplace and talk about the spiritual principles but the challenge is that you might not be able to quote scriptures in the place. You can state what the scriptures say in layman's words without making it "thus, saith the Lord." This is where you have to use wisdom just as you have seen, learned and heard me do in this class to make a point about ministering in the workplace.

If you are in the work environment and you cannot share your Christian faith, then you have to let your students know that you are a Christian and that you have learned a lot of wisdom that helped you to become successful in what you do. For example, you can share how positive things have happened to you as a result of some very healthy principles that you live by. Exhort the student to strive for integrity, good moral values, honesty, etc., and include "inspirational time" in your classroom teaching sessions. You do not have to quote scriptures at them but you can open the floor at the end of class for those that will want to learn how to apply some of the godly principles in their lives. You can then meet outside of the workplace with those who are interest in receiving an impartation from you. This meeting can then be your impartation or activation session outside of the workplace. For instance, you can say, "Let's all get up and believe that as we get up, we are challenging ourselves to reach for higher heights and as a result, will be endued with the ability to go forth to prosper, to be motivated, to be all that we can be, etc." You do not have to mention the Lord's name but you can privately ask the Lord to endue them with power from on High before class. Always remember that God loves them and wants to reach them even with the

slightest open door that they give Him. Therefore, what you do is stand in the gap for them before God.

Chapter 4

Goal Setting and Defining the Nature of the Mentoring Relationship

This is where the mentor needs to take the lead in setting forth some things in the relationship. One of those things that needs to be in place is for the mentor to establish what would be the duties of the mentor and what would be the duties of the mentee. This helps you both agree on what the final outcome of the mentoring relationship should be.

I like implementation and I like to see fruits. Therefore, I advise you to let the mentee know that whatever the two of you agree upon, you also commit to do. The mentor should desire to see an active step in accomplishing what was agreed upon with the mentee. As I said before, there are times that things happen that are not within our control and the mentor should be sympathetic when such things happen in the life of the mentee but the mentee should not fall into the pattern of using his or her life events as excuses over and over again.

Giving and Receiving Feedbacks:

You need to also establish how feedbacks are to be given by the mentor and received by the mentee. This means that both the mentor and mentee have to agree on the system of feedback that they choose and the mentee has to be willing to receive feedback from the mentor. It will be a waste of the mentor's time to take on someone that they cannot speak into his or her life or give feedback to. If you are one that gets offended when your mentor gives you feedback, then you are not ready for mentoring. You cannot afford to be someone who wears his or her feelings on the sleeve or gets easily hurt when your mentor speaks to you.

One of the things that I say to a new mentee is, "do not wear your feelings on your sleeve" because mentoring requires that you make some changes in your life. Some of the changes might not be easy depending on where you have been in life but if you are going to live a godly life, then you have to be willing to be conformed to the image of Christ. Feedback or speaking into your life does not mean that your mentor is to criticize, wound or hurt you by what he or she says to you, but to give you real good input that will help you develop in your Christian walk. Therefore, feedback should be encouraged and given in love. The mentee needs to be aware that there are times that love has to be tough especially when the mentee is rebellious, stubborn or in great sin and is unwilling to change.

Getting Permission from Your Mentee:

In my mentoring class, I make the student sign a permission slip for me to speak into their lives. They also sign a permission slip for me to give them feedback. Therefore, you as the mentee need to give your mentor permission to speak into your life and permission to give you feedback. I for one will not take it upon me to speak as a mentor into the life of someone who will not give me permission to speak into his or her life. The reason is because, if I cannot speak into the life of my mentee, then my mentoring him or her is of no use. Get the mentee's written permission to speak into his or her life. This is vital because you do not want to give feedback to your mentee and have him or her tell you off because there was no strategy set forth on how you are to speak into his or her life or give feedback. For instance, if you have a mentee who insists on dressing like a *"hoochie"* and you try to help her out in a loving way, but she continually says to you, "That is who I am," you will have to come up with a strategy on how to deal with the situation. This strategy will include an effective feedback plan.

You are not to pretend that the mentee does not have a problem especially if she insists on exposing everything about her body parts and is being accused of going after other people's husbands. If a person is being accused of the same thing everywhere he or she goes, chances are that there is some validity in the accusations. I will not tell such a person, "Bless your little heart, you are just fine the way you are." Instead, I will let her know in a very loving way to change the way she dresses. I will tell her to take a good look in the mirror and then tell herself that she truly wants to be the type of lady that every cheap guy is looking for on the street. I will also tell her that she may not be that type of a "free-for-all-lady," but the way that she dresses and the way that she presents herself to the people out there speaks volumes. I will let her know that she is advertising her body so if she wants to keep the flies away, then she needs to dress differently.

If the person is unwilling to change, you need to find out if the person really needs mentoring or not. Who wants to be in a process that does not bear fruits? I will seek the Lord and if He says OK to let the person go, I will tell the mentee, "I can't hang, I'm sorry, I've tried but it seems as if you do not need my help." I will tell the mentee that I am releasing him or her to the Lord because there maybe another mentor out there for him or her but I know that I am not the one.

Be Honest with Your Mentor/Mentee:

You need to make sure that your mentor knows about the things that you are dealing with in your life that might impact the mentoring relationship. Let the mentor know about your circumstances. For instance, let your mentor know if you are living in a home where the members do not like visitors or if you are in a home where your spouse is not a believer. Let your mentor know if you cannot meet with him or her regularly because of your living situation; just be honest. Honesty is very, very critical to the success of your mentoring relationship. Just like any other relationship, if you are going to make it successful, you have to be willing to work at it.

I already told you in Chapter 2 that you are to find some materials that will help you get a basic understanding of what mentoring is about. Basically, in mentoring we need a lot of patience. There are some godly qualities that I look for in a person and if I do not see the qualities in a person and if the person is not willing to develop these godly qualities, I do not waste my time with the person for too long. Therefore, I have a word for the mentee. If you desire mentoring, you must be teachable, you must be correctable and you must be leadable. This does not mean that you have to be a puppet or that you have to be subservient, but it means that you must be willing to take or heed the godly counsel that comes to you through your mentor. If you do not understand something, ask and get clarification but be willing to discuss issues with your mentor. Do not insist in your wrong ways. If you have done something and someone comes up to you and you know that it is not the first person that has brought that character flaw to your attention, do not be defensive but be willing to change. If you need deliverance, then be honest with your mentor so that your mentor can send you to a deliverance ministry where you can get delivered. You must be leadable and you have to know when to give honor to whom honor is due.

The mentor has to give realistic input and let the mentee know if he or she is going to call him or her over the phone. Some people do not like to communicate over the phone, they prefer for you to meet with them face to face. Others do not mind communication over the phone or through the email. This why you and your mentee must agree on how feedback is to be given and received. Try to handle negative feedbacks with love and care. This does not mean that your feedbacks are to be constantly negative when they do not need to be. Try to encourage your mentee in a positive way because some people might get discouraged if all they hear is just negative feedback.

Also, you have to establish the nature and times of contact. As I stated in Chapter 3, some mentoring relationships might be long distance. So, do not let it discourage you when someone calls you from Washington, D.C. and you are here in Georgia and the person wants you to mentor him or her. Do not say, "How am I going to mentor you while you are all the way over there? I'm not coming to Washington, D.C." You do not have to go to Washington, D.C. to mentor the person. You can mentor over the phone or through email. You and your mentee can decide if there is ever going to be a face to face meeting. For instance, you can decide OK, send me your reasons for needing a mentor and tell me the areas in which you need my help. Even though the mentee is quite a distance from you, you can help him or her to understand what mentoring is all about and then get an insight into what he or she is doing. You can guide this person each step of the way to where he or she needs to be spiritually. Your goal is always to develop a plan of how you can best help him or her to get to the next level.

Duration of Your Mentoring Relationship:

You as the mentor must establish the duration or the length of time of the mentoring relationship. For example, I am in a mentoring relationship with my students for the next six months. It is a boundary that I have set for our mentoring relationship. We can extend the duration later but for now, it is scheduled to end in six months. This way nobody gets hurt if they can no longer have access to me as they used to during our mentoring relationship. It does not mean that I will cut them off forever but it means that there will be a change in our relationship. If you do not establish the duration of the mentoring relationship and your mentee begins to view you as best friend, they just might get hurt when the mentoring relationship comes to an end or you might shock them when you bring the mentoring relationship to an end. The mentee might go away hurt and wounded because he or she cannot understand why it now takes you a week to return his or her call.

You have to be prepared for when the God-given grace for the mentoring relationship is over. Therefore, I prefer that you set a length of time for the mentoring period. For instance, tell your mentee, "I will mentor you for three months, for six months or even for one year. After the initial mentoring period is over, we can then revisit the relationship to see if it is still what God wants for you." You want this type of arrangement with your mentee because if it turns out that God is moving you on to other things, you have not pinned yourself or backed yourself into a corner that you cannot get out of without wounding your mentee. You and your mentee both have to be available for the next thing that God wants to do with you and for you by not over committing yourself to a prolonged mentoring relationship that God has not committed you to.

Need to Renegotiate New Mentoring Season:
It is better for you to extend or to add another six months each time the agreed duration is over and this should only be if the mentee still needs input from you. The extension of a mentoring relationship must be discussed by the mentor and the mentee. It is better for you as the mentor to do this rather than have a mentee that you have not seen for three years say, "you are my mentor" and

then call you up out of the blue or come around thinking that you are to always be available to meet with him or her because, after all, you are their mentor. So, make sure that you set the duration for mentoring.

One of the things that you should probably do, is let the mentee know when your mutually agreed upon mentoring season is coming to an end as this will help kill any codependency that may have been building up. If the person has become attached to you and he or she does not want the mentoring relationship to end, then you will have to say to him or her, let us go back to the Lord because He is the one that sets the mentoring plans. Therefore, let us see what He is saying about our mentoring relationship right now. When the mentee's desire is bordering on ungodly attachment, you might need the Lord to deliver you from the situation. This is why I always warn the mentor not to be swept into a codependency situation where even if the mentoring is over, the person is still calling you every week at midnight.

Short and Long Term Goals:

You want to establish short term goals and long term goals with your mentee. As I stated before, the duration of my mentoring season with the students in my mentoring class is six months and my short term goal for them is to see them grow in areas of their lives in which they have been previously hindered or challenged by the enemy. I want to see Christ-like characters and a good understanding of what ministry is about. My long term goal for them is that at the end of their mentoring season with me, they should be able to instruct others concerning mentoring. This means that they should be able to take someone under their wings; either on a one-on-one basis, through email, or over the phone and mentor the person. They should be able to give others directives concerning mentoring. The information that they received from my classroom instructions should serve as a solid platform for them to be able to instruct others in any classroom setting.

As I stated before, **the principle of the kingdom is give and it shall be given unto you.** You can always use this textbook and the accompanying manual as the instructional materials for the students. The students can use the manual to follow along as you the mentor is teaching them in a classroom. For instance, you can have the students read lesson one and you can come together afterwards in a classroom to fully discuss everything that was outlined in the lesson. You can do the same for the next lesson until you have gone through all the lessons in the manual with your students. You should always make room for what the Holy Spirit brings into each lesson that is uniquely needed by the students. Therefore, you should seek more revelations from the Lord concerning your particular class or your students. Also, be quick to recognize and discern what the Lord is saying concerning each one of your mentees.

I expect every single person that has been through this mentoring course to be able to mentor other people. One of the things that is not being done in the body of Christ today is raising up people through mentoring. People just come to church and they are not given any guidelines to help them in areas that they struggle with sin or personal habits. Sometimes church members will go to a small group outside church premises for fellowship but still no guidelines. Some churches do not even have small groups for people to go to. Therefore, mentoring gives you an opportunity to be responsible for someone else for a season. You can then impart into the person the things that you have learned that have aided your spiritual growth. Basically, mentoring gives you an opportunity to give back to those in need.

Accountability Enforced:

Accountability is a good thing and God holds each one of us accountable for what we do. He rewards a lot of the good things that we do. Mentoring allows you to also hold people accountable. It allows you to help people see the things in their lives that are so visible to everyone else except the people. It is done in love and for godly reasons. For example, Gina and I went to visit someone that I had been mentoring for some months and we were shocked at the state of her house. It was a very beautifully designed house and it was not even up to 6 years old yet, but the lady and her daughter left it like a pig's pen. I told her that God has given her a beautiful, beautiful house but she and her daughter were abusing it. I told them that there is no reason why they should so neglect their house; especially since they are not sick. I was firm with them and I told them that if she and her daughter do not like cleaning, then, she should get a cleaning lady because I know that she can afford it. The state of this house was so bad that when you step into the kitchen areas and the staircase, you literally have to cover your eyes because of the ugly and nasty stains that assault your eyes. If anything was spillable, it had been spilled on the rug and on the walls. There were green, yellow, red and brown stains all over this house that was supposed to have been so beautiful. I was in shock about the state of this house.

I held her and her daughter accountable as stewards of what God has already given to them. I told them that they cannot continue in the state of mess that they were in because they are supposed to be living testimonies not just outside but inside the house. As women of God, our houses should testify about the goodness of God when people walk into them. Your house testifies as to what God has done for you but if you make it look like a pig's pen, then people will say, "I can't believe the condition of their home. What is wrong with them? Are they not supposed to be Christians?" I say to you that God likes clean environments.

Therefore, when you see your mentee going the wrong way, you can in a nice way tell him or her to make some necessary changes. If your male mentee is walking around with his pants dropping down his buttocks, you can gently tell him to pull his pants up. If the mentee tells you that the younger guys now wear their pants this way, then, give him a little education of how the whole culture of wearing pants below the buttock is a gay culture that came straight out of prison! When I tell people about where the culture came from, they are shocked. My little nephew that visited from outside the country was shocked to hear that wearing pants below the buttocks was a gay culture from prison. He told me that he had his pants back home that he wears below his buttocks but his little eyes popped wide open when he heard where the culture came from. I asked him if he was advertising his buttocks for male homosexuals and he said, "NO," so I said, "Then, pull your pants up when you get home!"

Policy on Phone Calls:

I said it before that in a mentoring relationship, it is very necessary for you to set boundaries. You really have to set boundaries because you don't want your mentee to call you at 11 pm or 12 midnight or wake you up at 2 am or 6 am and when you talk to him or her, it is nothing about nothing. In other words, it is the same old story about his or her situation that he or she is not willing to do something about. Therefore, it is necessary for you to let your mentee know your set time for phone calls. If it is once a week or once a month, let them know because you don't want people usurping all your time and making what you are supposed to be doing to help them become a noose on your neck that is trying to choke you. Therefore, tell your mentee your policy about phone calls.

For instance, you may say, I have a policy of no calls after 10 pm and no calls on the weekend. If you take calls on the weekend or if you only take calls on Saturday during the weekend, be sure to let your mentee know. You can then hold your mentee accountable when he or she goes beyond the boundary that you two have set. Enforcing this policy may also help to give you an insight into the character of your mentee because if he or she disregards your policy or instructions and develops a negative attitude, then, you can safely surmise that the flesh is still very much in control of the mentee's life. It also tells you who needs to go back into God's fiery furnace for a while and get cooked a little bit for some impurities (flesh) to drop off.

Be honest about what you as the mentor will not allow in the relationship, i.e., do not call me after 9 or 10 pm and do not call me at midnight. We had a lady that used to bug me and one day she called me from a motel here in Atlanta at about 2 am asking to come to my house. She and I have talked about her situation several times before but she was not willing to change. She has had situations involving other people's spouses before and I had tried to get her to make some changes in her lifestyle but she ignored my advice. She was in one of such situations again and she had checked into a motel the day before.

I wanted to know if she was in danger and she was not because it was the same old story. I wanted to know if she knew what time it was and she did. She was well aware that she was calling me at 2 am and she did not care. I think that it is very disrespectful of a person's time and sleep to call them up at 2 am when you are not going through a crisis and you are not in any danger. She came to see me later that day and from my conversation with her, I could see that she enjoyed being a victim rather than making some lifestyle changes. She turned out to be one of those women who believe that all they have to do is to wait for God to give them a rich husband because she said to me, "Why should I go get a job when God can just give me a rich husband?" I said, "Really, you are talking to someone who works. I am not just sitting down saying, OK, God all I need is just a rich husband right now." I told her that when she finds that rich man, he will most likely be looking for a woman who is godly and has her act together. After all, who wants a looser as a life partner?

Questions and Answers Time with Your Mentee:

Set the atmosphere in such a way that your mentee can feel free to ask you questions when he or she has questions. Do not give them the impression that you know what you do not know. Again, I say to you that if your mentee should ask you a question to which you do not know the answer, either tell him or her that you do not know the answer but you can look into it and get back with him or her, or you can direct him or her to where they can find the answer. These days, you can get a write up on just about any topic you put on the internet so make use of the internet to find answers to questions about secular issues.

If it is something from the scripture, then, do a Bible search to see what the answer is from scriptures. If it is something that requires divine revelation, then, you and your mentee can fast and pray so that the Lord can give you the answer. As I stated before, always remember that there is no question that is too difficult for God and with God all things are possible.

Preparing the Mentee for Future Results:

Make sure that you let your mentee know what you hope to see in him or her at the end of the mentoring season. If he or she is not willing to change according to God's direction through you, you can tell him or her that they are barking up the wrong tree because you have a plan to see some positive results in them. Otherwise, you will be wasting your time and effort on someone who is not willing to change and follow God's plan for him or her. Such people come up to you and while you are trying to help them, they are full of all kinds of excuses. They are not making any progress in their Christian walk and if you do not confront them, they will just take up your time for nothing. If at the end of your mentoring season there is no result, you will have to let them go rather than go around the mountain with them again without fruits. Letting your mentee know that you desire results will help you to give him or her, the final feedback of whether or not you made a wise investment with your time in him or her. You and your mentee can discuss the results at the end of the mentoring season.

Ask your mentee what he or she would like to see in him or herself at the end of the mentoring season because when the mentee commits to the desired result, you can then give feedback on whether or not the result is beginning to manifest. Always let your mentee know that you desire to see him or her manifest the results that you have both agreed upon because no one wants to do something and not see the effort produce results. Being fruitful is part of the commandment that God gave us and the Lord Jesus told us that those who are not fruitful will actually be cast away. We see this in **John 15: 1-2:**

> **"I am the true vine, and my Father
> is the husbandman. *2* <u>Every</u> <u>branch</u>**

**in me that beareth not fruit he
taketh away: and every branch that
beareth fruit, he purgeth it, that it
may bring forth more fruit."**

Also, when the Lord Jesus came to a fig tree in **Matthew
21:18-19** and the tree had no fruits, what did Jesus do? He
cursed the fig tree.

**"Now in the morning as he returned
into the city, he hungered. *19* And
when he saw a fig tree in the way,
he came to it, and found nothing
thereon, but leaves only, and said
unto it, Let no fruit grow on thee
henceforward for ever."**

We are called to bring forth fruits for God's kingdom
and you can tell when somebody is a visionary and
produces fruits. Some people have a clear understanding
of who they are in Christ even if they do not know what
they are supposed to be doing and they have a hunger
and they want to do something for the kingdom. But
you have others who do nothing because they believe
that they are the victim of where they have been, how
they were born and what happen to them in the past.
Therefore, they have no vision and are not willing to
have a vision. They have become satisfied with being a
victim. You can easily discern these types of people as
you begin your mentoring relationship.

Impartation/Activation Session
You should make time to meet with your mentee so

that you can impart to him or her, the anointing that the Lord has given you. Therefore, there is a need for you to lay your hands on your mentee to impart the grace that is upon your life. I said in the previous chapters that you ought to do this because both you and your mentee need the grace of God to succeed in your mentoring relationship. If you have not done this exercise as outlined in the previous chapters, then you need to come together with your mentee so that you can perform the laying on of hands. You need to ask the Lord to release through you to your mentee, the grace to be able to receive from you, to be teachable, correctable and leadable. Also, ask the Lord to impart to your mentee the spiritual gifts that he or she needs from you.

One of the things that the Lord always encourages me to do is to lay hands on the people that I am working with because sometimes when you lay hands on people, because of the virtue that is in you, you can actually release that virtue to them. For instance, I walk in the deliverance anointing and there have been instances that some very stubborn spirits have been driven away by my laying hands on or making contact with the people that they afflict. Usually, the deaf and dumb spirits will leave the people as you lay hands and as a result, the people begin to hear what God is saying to them or the Word of God can now begin to make sense to them. Many people have said that they are now seeing and hearing from the Lord for the first time because the demon of spiritual blindness and the demons of deaf and dumbness that had them bound left after my laying hands on them.

Therefore, lay hands on your mentee with his or her permission. In one of my books titled, **How to Discern and Expel Evil Spirits**, I shared a story about how it was very difficult for me to get saved because of the deaf and dumb spirits that had blocked my ears from hearing the truth of the Word of God. It was only when a Spirit-filled Christian laid her hands on me that the spirits fled and I got saved two days later! Before this time, my mother and some other members of her church had tried unsuccessfully to get me to give my life to Jesus. One Sunday, I looked at how sad my Mom was as the pastor was making an alter call and I was not responding. I decided to appease her by answering the alter call. I knew it would get her off my back. All of us that answered the alter call were taken to another room outside the sanctuary. Below is an excerpt of the event as I narrated it on pages 34-36 of my book *How to Discern and Expel Evil Spirits*:

> *We were taken out of the sanctuary into another room. When I got into the room, I was assigned to a lady to talk to me. At this time, I did not know that I was demon possessed but I was well dressed and I was looking good! The lady I was assigned to said to me, "Oh, after I finish praying for you, you're going to become a saint." You never say that to a Roman Catholic person because the way we were taught about becoming a saint when I was a Catholic is that for you to be a saint, you have to have lived and died. After 200 years, the Pope tells them to dig up your bones and they will then pronounce you a saint after examining all your good deeds. To my knowledge, that was how they made saints. Therefore, I found it absurd for the lady to tell me that she was going to make me a saint! I looked at her and said: "You make me a saint, you?" She said, "Yes." (God is really laughing now because He remembers that incident!) I said, "I am sorry, I am sorry*

for you and I am sorry for whoever has been putting those ideas in your head that you can make someone a saint, but I think I'm in the wrong place!" So I turned around and was about to walk off and she said, "You're not going to pray to receive salvation?" And I said, "Not if you're going to make me a saint!" She asked me, "You're leaving?" And I said, "Watch me!"

I could still see this lady and her desperation to get through to me that I needed to get saved. She did not want to grab me because it would appear too forceful. She did not know how to get it into my "demon-laden head" at that time that I needed salvation; that I was barely making it. Not knowing what else to do, she ran after me as I was about to leave the room and I looked at her and I saw that she was very concerned about me as though I was going to drop dead the next minute. She said to me, "Well, since you don't want to get saved, can I pray for you?" And I said, "Of course." Roman Catholics always go to get prayed for so I did not mind her praying for me as long as she did not try to make me a saint. She took my hands and she prayed for me. When I got back into the sanctuary, my mom asked me, "Did you get saved?" I said, "No, because the lady did not know how to make a saint. Why would I let somebody who is ignorant about how someone becomes a saint get me saved?" She said, "You didn't get saved? I said, "No." This happened at the Sunday service. Do you know that the

Tuesday of that week I got saved?

I do not think my Mom thought there was any hope for me after the above incident but God moved just two days later. What I did not know then was that my agreement for the lady to hold my hands while she was praying for me was my first consenting touch by a Spirit-filled Christian. The Tuesday of that week, I got saved because it was the Lord's divine appointment for my salvation. My mother made an appointment for me to go and say goodbye to the pastor because I was leaving to come back to the USA that weekend but unknown to her I agreed to go see the pastor for another reason. I wanted to see the pastor in order to have a serious talk with him about the 10% tithes that he was taking from my mother. Needless to say that before I left the meeting with the pastor, I was a born again Christian! The Lord later showed me that the deaf and dumb demons had their fingers plugged in my ears so that I could not hear the Word of God that was coming to me. Therefore, whenever someone tried to talk to me about the Lord, I would just debate the person. It did not matter what the person said, I had the counter argument because I was a philosophy student for a while. According to the Lord, having hands laid on me by a Spirit-filled Christian drove away the demons and paved the way for me to get saved two days later.

Therefore, I say again, lay hands on your mentee and ask the Lord to release to the mentee the gifts and the things that He has placed within you that might help the mentee to get to where they need to be. Be willing to release the anointing to those that God has given you to mentor. Do not lay hands on your mentee if you feel a check in your spirit about him or her. So, continue to learn some basic things about your mentee such as commitment to a project, integrity, good ethics, etc., and do not ignore warning signs that might show laziness, lack of integrity, low moral values, emotional instability, codependence tendency, etc. Also, do not forget the duration of your mentoring relationship. This means that you have to avoid loose ends in your mentoring relationship. If you committed to six months, fulfill your six months commitment but at the same time when your six months are coming up, make sure that you have a solid exit strategy before you get locked into another season of mentoring that you have not bargained for. **This does not mean that you are not to have contact with your former mentees. It just means the time you committed to for a formal mentoring relationship is over.**

Again, ask the Lord to show you how you can take your relationship with your mentee to another level and always ask the Lord continually to reveal to you ways that you can spiritually and physically help your mentee. You might have some areas that your mentee might also be able to help you. For instance, Jack is coming to help us mow the lawn next week. It is actually a give and take relationship because the fact that you are the mentor does not mean that the mentee does not know something that might be beneficial to you spiritually and physically. There are some things that you might learn from or that you might receive by listening to him or her that might open your eyes to some spiritual truths. Therefore, do not feel lofty and disregard the spiritual gifts that are in your mentee.

<u>Note</u>: *Remember that these materials were first presented in actual classroom settings.*

Question and Answer Session
Cindy: What if the person is seeking your wisdom,

your understanding and your help and you perceive that you are going to be the person's mentor and that the person is going to be your mentee but the person is not used to the mentor/mentee terms? So, how would you put it so that it can have the structure of what we call mentoring? Will we meet, pray together and still do all that you outlined but may not use the mentor/mentee terms?

Mary: If the person is not in the church for instance, you might not be able to use the terms with the person but if it is someone you feel like you are comfortable enough to speak to, what you can do is say to the person, "There is a term for what you are asking me to do. You are asking me for a mentoring relationship with you." This type of request should actually open the door for you to help the person understand something about mentoring. For instance, if someone comes to me and says, "Mary, I feel like the Lord is calling me into ministry and I have been watching you and **I really want to get trained** by someone (see the words the person is using—get trained) who knows what they are doing or someone that God is using in ministry. I want to be trained by someone who knows what ministry is about." I will listen to find out what the person is really requiring from me. I might or might not mentor the person depending on what the Lord says but I do not believe that everybody has to go out there and make mistakes in order to learn.

My belief is that we can all learn from other people's mistakes. If there are things that I have learned that might keep another person from making the same type of mistakes that I made, I am willing to help the person but you define for them what they are asking you to do. Therefore, when someone says to you, "I want you to do ... for me," then you should say, "What you are asking me to do is called mentoring." I for one might even take it a step further by telling the person that I have a book about mentoring that might be beneficial to him or her. I will pray to hear from the Lord on the matter but meanwhile, I might say to the person, "I need to pray to find out if the Lord is calling me to train (mentor) you so I will call you later so that we can get together to discuss the matter." I will tell the person to also pray. When I meet with the person, I can then open the topic up for discussion and let the Lord work between the two of us so that I can either confirm that yes, the Lord is leading me to work with this person or no, it is not the Lord's will for me to mentor the person.

The bottom line is that you need to tell the person that the two of you need to pray about the matter in order to see what the Lord wants. You do not want to jump into something and then find out that God is not in it because if God is not in it, you might be crying out to the Lord to save you at the end. You might be like Peter in the water crying, "Lord save me." He is gracious; He will deliver us when we cry out to Him but we do not always have to make a mess of things. Since the person is new and does not have any knowledge about mentoring, you might also have to help him or her obtain some materials on mentoring. You can even show the person some of the resources that you have. You can emphatically tell the person that mentoring takes time, it takes commitment and it takes a willingness to come together to invest for the next six months to a year to do... I told you before that in the workplace, mentoring is called coaching. Some people might not even know the word mentoring and all they know is that they want you to train them or help them learn what they need to learn so that they can accomplish their desires.

Steve: My question is what is the difference between counseling and conversation?

Mary: Well, we all sometimes call the people we know or each other and during our normal conversations, we can tell the person we are talking to about our problems. For instance, the conversation might go something like this, "I have this problem, what do you think should be my normal course of action?" The person may give you godly advice or spiritual counsel if he or she is Spirit-filled. On the other hand, when someone is having deep emotional issues, deep mental issues, serious drug issues or serious marital issues to the point of contemplating a divorce, you have to be very careful about what you tell the person because the situation might be way out of your league if you are not a trained counselor. If you are not an ordained minister or a trained Christian counselor, you might give the wrong counsel and if the person should follow through with your counsel, the person can get into serious mental or physical trouble and you can get into trouble also as a result. Although we carry the Holy Spirit within us as Christians, we do not want to give the wrong prescription in areas that require specific training and licensing. This is why you should always refer people to ordained ministers or professional Christian counselors. Most pastors and Christian Counselors are endowed by God to help people deal with the crisis of life so make use of their expertise because you do not want to be on the six o'clock news as a quack doctor responsible for a calamity or being charged with a criminal offence because of your wrong counsel.

Remember the church that was in the news in Atlanta because the pastor said that "parents and church leaders can beat foolishness out of a rebellious child?" The incident played out in the media because parents took that as a license to begin spanking their children publicly in their attempts to discipline them. As you listened to the story, it was clear that the pastor preached a sermon that, **"Foolishness is bound in the heart of a child; but the rod of correction shall drive it far from him"** (Proverbs 22:15). The pastor admitted preaching this scripture as a tool for disciplining rebellious children. According to the media account, driving out foolishness from the head of the children in the church got to the point of child abuse and it seemed as if everybody caught the vision that foolishness was bound up in the head of the rebellious children in the church. Therefore, they were all driving it out with the rod except that they all ended up on the six o'clock news as the worst church in Atlanta. The question was how well did the church members observe the Spirit of the Word of God in **Proverbs 22:15**? Did discipline truly turn into abuse? You do not want to say something to someone that they might use as criteria to do something that is against the law.

If your mentee really needs professional help, which is what I believe your question is addressing, again, refer him or her to a trained Christian counselor, a Christian psychologist, medical doctor, etc. If during the course of talking to your mentee you discover that the demon of rejection has pinned him or her down and he or she can not seem to get out of that pit, refer him or her to a deliverance ministry that can help. If you do not know of a deliverance ministry, ask around and if necessary inform your mentee that you were unable to find a deliverance ministry in the area where you both live but you will continue to look for one for him or her.

Although this is not directly related to counseling, I will add that if when you were talking to your mentee during one of your meetings you discern that one of the mentee's problems is that he or she does not understand scriptures or the application of scriptures, then refer him or her to a good Bible study group. If for instance someone does not know how to flow in the gifts of the Spirit, a prophetic church like Life Center Ministries in Atlanta is a good place to refer the person for training in the prophetic. You can not do it all for your mentee. Do not become a *Jack of all Trades.*

You have to know your own limitation as a mentor. Godly advice or wisdom is very valuable to us all as Christians; we still have to know that we cannot operate in professions that we have not been trained or licensed to operate in legally. If on the other hand you are an ordained minister or a trained counselor, then feel free to practice your profession according to the law. You do not want to say something that is quoted out of context and have your name attached to it. Trained counselors help their clients to understand what they are saying to them. **You have to decide where to draw the line between godly advice and a directive for a cause of action in a legal or medical situation and always keep in mind the legal implication concerning counseling.**

Elaine: This is concerning the market place. Can you lay hands silently and if you do lay hands without their knowledge (though you are a Christians doing it) would it be witchcraft?

Mary: I like the scripture that says, **"Lay hands suddenly on no man, neither be partaker of other men's sins: keep thyself pure"** (1 Timothy 5:22). You will notice that whenever people came to Jesus some of them would be blind as bats as they come to Him. They would say to Him, "Lord, help us" and He would reply, "What do you want me to do for you?" When you are not well versed in scriptures; I know for myself when I was not well versed in scriptures, I would say, "What is wrong with Jesus? This person is blind; what else would he want from You Lord?" As I got to know the Lord and His Word, I realized that if He had laid hands suddenly on a blind man and his blindness was cured, the man could have been upset because his blindness was his means of sustenance; that is what he used to beg for alms! Therefore, a blind person's plea for help could be asking Him for alms and if the Lord should presumptuously heal him, he could become upset with the Lord for healing his eyes and taking away his money making tool! Therefore, the Lord was not presumptuous. Instead, He asked everyone what they wanted from Him.

As a result, of the above scripture and the way the Lord operated His ministry, I always ask people if it is alright for me to lay hands on them. I will not lay my hands on any man or woman without his or her permission. Therefore, I say to you that if they do not give you permission to lay hands on them and you lay hands on them, you might do more than just violate their rights. You might invite such a powerful warfare against yourself that the Lord will have to deliver you before you become a casualty of ignorance in the devil's hand. God does not violate our will and what makes us different from angels and other creature is our free will. He told me that a person has a right to go to hell if that is what the person chooses. A person has a right to keep their demons if that is what the person chooses. You are not God in other people's lives because they have the right to say NO to anything that you say to them that they do not want. It is their God-given will to say YES or NO. We must all obey that.

You see how God set it up? If you do not want to get saved, He does not force you. We cannot go beyond the will of a person. The following is an incident that the Lord used to teach me to respect a person's will:

As an intercessor, I was attending a prayer meeting one day and the prayer meeting was

133

being held in the basement of the church that I belonged to at the time. I got into the church and was going downstairs to the basement when I ran into another intercessor. She was a mother of two and she was also on the staircase and was going down to the basement as well. She had her nine month old baby across her chest in a sling and a huge diaper bag in her left arm and was holding on to her three year old daughter with her right hand. I immediately felt sorry for her and I thought; now, here is this mother with two children and a huge diaper bag going down the staircase. As a good and dedicated Christian, I was ready to help her so I said to her, "Let me help you with your little girl (the three year old)." I picked up the little girl and we came down to the bottom of the stairs. When I set the little girl down, she let out a cry as though someone had seriously injured her. She screamed and she cried, she looked at me, she looked at her mother and she was furious. Her mother and I looked at each other because we did not know what was wrong with her. To our amazement, she defiantly went up the staircase by herself and then proceeded to come down by herself. When she came down, she immediately stopped crying. Her mother was so embarrassed and apologized to me for her daughter's behavior. I told her that I was OK and she does not have to worry about it. When I got into the prayer room, I immediately lowered my head and quietly asked the Lord what had just happened concerning the little girl. The

Lord said to me, "You violated her will; as little as she is (3 years old), she already has a will and she knows when her will has been violated. She had a desire to go down the staircase by herself without being carried but in your zeal to help her, you took it away from her and she reacted. This is why I do not override any of your will down there. I never violate anyone's will."

As you can imagine, I was shocked to learn how we can easily violate other people's will in our eagerness to help them. I learned from the above experience that even if it is a little three year old, he or she has a will and you have to get the child's or the parent's permission. **Do not just go out there and be the savior of the world all by yourself by laying hands on people without their permission.** You are going to get smacked by the devil big time if you do. Also, if you went and laid hands secretly on a person in your class without his or her permission, you might unleash the spirits of revenge and retaliation against you from the person. The devil will try to strike you back because he knows that you operated without the person's permission.

If you are a seer like me, you will see at night that not only the demons in the person will come after you but every foul spirit that works through the person. They will all be at your house that night. The evil spirits in the person might even solicit the help of other wicked spirits that are in the people that hate you. These people might be your family members, past acquaintances, colleagues, etc., and they will all piggyback on the spirits in that person as they come to war against you. It is amazing how the devil likes to use it as an opportunity for revenge. It becomes a big open door for evil spirits to put out a war cry of "whosoever will," please, come and help us fight against this person. I was shocked at how even the spirits in some members of my family were soliciting other wicked spirits to come and help them fight against me when I laid hands on someone who was demon possessed without his permission. This is why I never, lay hands on someone who has not given me permission. You can pray for people but do not touch them without their permission. Another thing that makes it really bad is that the evil spirits know that the Lord wars in righteousness and that He will not violate His Word in order to defend you when you are in rebellion (laying hands on someone without permission) against His Word. Therefore, you can actually get yourself killed by evil spirits when you operate outside of God's Word or commandment.

> **"And I saw heaven opened, and behold a white horse; and he that sat upon him was called <u>Faithful</u> and <u>True</u>, <u>and in righteousness he doth judge and make war</u>"** (Revelation 19:11).

However, the Lord will move on your behalf when you repent of your rebellion. It is amazing how His grace covers us during our time of foolishness or operating in zeal without wisdom.

Chapter 5

The Act of Mentoring

This chapter deals with the actual act of mentoring another person and in particular, the duties or the role of the mentor concerning the mentee as well as the role of the mentee concerning the mentor. I start this chapter with the scripture in **Hebrews 5:13-14** that says:

> **"For <u>every one that useth milk is unskilful in the word of righteousness</u>: for he is a babe. <u>But strong meat belongeth to them that are of full age, even those who by reason of use have their senses exercised</u> to discern both good and evil."**

It is God's will that we grow and have our spiritual senses exercised so that we can discern between that which is good and that which is evil. This is where the mentor comes in to help the mentee to become skilled in the Word of righteousness and in the application of wisdom in order to develop and grow in the Lord. Therefore, it is the duty of the mentor to assess the level of spiritual maturity of the mentee before taking the initial step to develop him or her. You must know or have an idea of the spiritual state of your mentee. This means that you must determine if he or she is a babe in Christ or a well seasoned Christian. Mentoring is to help facilitate growth and maturity and if you are going to help someone in this area, then you must know the person's current state.

As I stated before in Chapter 3, a person cannot grow beyond his or her level of understanding of the Word of God. I also stated that the key scripture that tells us this is **3 John 1:2** and that our physical prosperity which includes our physical growth is directly tied to our spiritual prosperity according to this scripture:

> **"Beloved, I wish above all things that thou mayest prosper and be in health, even as thy soul prospereth."**

This means therefore, that everyone of us must make sure that his or her soul is prospering so that we can prosper in the physical things as well. This is also why God told Joshua in **Joshua 1:8**:

> **"This book of the law shall not depart out of thy mouth; but thou shalt meditate therein day and night, that thou mayest observe to do according to all that is written therein: for then thou shalt make thy way prosperous, and then thou shalt have good success."**

Therefore, the mentor needs to know the mentee's level of understanding of God's Word, biblical principles and the application of biblical principles or wisdom. Knowing this will help you to determine where to begin to help your mentee. The mentor also needs to assess the mentee's level of development in areas that will directly impact the growth of the mentee. Some of these areas are character, integrity, commitment to relationships, commitment to projects, moral values/godly principles, financial management, business or work ethics, dress code and general outlook in life. You need to know what is the mentee's governing principle or motivating factor in life. Is the mentee a victim or a victor?

I know that there are some people out there that when you plan something with them, they will pull a "no-show-no-call" on you and when they see you, they do not think that it is important enough to say anything about what they did and they act as though it never happened. Therefore, if you have a mentee whose character is shady and has no integrity, does not keep appointments, does not call to apologize for missing an appointment but glazes over issues with you, you cannot ignore him or her when you are the mentor because it is a serious character flaw. You must take note of this type of behavior and know when to confront your mentee about the character flaw.

There are also people with very low moral values, poor work ethics and poor financial management skills. When you talk to some of these people, you will discover that some of them once had a financial settlement of about sixty thousand to a hundred thousand dollars but blew it all within one to four years. If you should ask them what they bought with the money, you will discover that they cannot account for anything useful that they did or obtained with the money. Some of them went and started leasing cars, living in motels, buying expensive jewelry, going on vacations or living from one town to another. With these types of people, you can immediately discern that they have no financial management skills and therefore, will need your input in this area.

Those who are caught up in ungodly lifestyles may need help in different areas, such as wisdom on how to get out of their current living arrangement, securing employment, referral to a professional Christian counselor or programs that might help them to kick a drug or promiscuous habit. Therefore, you have to know where people that you are mentoring are coming from and if they are bound up in a life of vice and you need to get an insight of what brought them to their current condition to begin with. Was it lust, slothfulness, desire to get rich quick, idleness or just poor management skills?

The insight you get will help you to know exactly the areas that you need to hold them accountable. Since you have their permission to speak into their lives, you can look at their character in order to either challenge them to do better in areas that they are lacking or send them to get help from the professionals. As I stated before, one of the major reasons for mentoring another person is to help the person develop godly character, integrity, good values, etc., so that the person can grow to fulfill their God-given destiny. Therefore, the mentor should be willing to challenge the mentee to grow in the areas the he or she sees the mentee as coming short. The mentor should also be willing to track the mentee's progress after each meeting. If after you have met with the mentee several times and he or she is still not demonstrating integrity but is still giving you flimsy excuses, you can firmly hold him or her accountable. You can tell the mentee that God does not like slothfulness and that God is looking for someone that has integrity.

I have told some people that one thing that keeps them from being used by God even though they are anointed and operate the gifts of the Spirit is their lack of integrity. One thing that I have learned from my walk with the Lord is that if He does not see integrity in you, He will sit you down on the bench like a ball player. He said to me one day, "Would you be willing to send someone to represent you knowing that the person will not faithfully represent you? Do you send them out to represent you when you know that they are going to do their own thing out there?" I said, "No" and He said, "Neither do I." This is one of the reasons that the Bible says in **Proverbs 20:6**:

> **"Most men will proclaim every one his own goodness: <u>but a faithful</u> man who can find?"**

God is looking for those that will faithfully represent His values, His character and His will. I will reemphasize again here that God set out in **Genesis 1:26** to make man in **His image** and **after His likeness** (character). This is why He said of David:

> **"... I have found David the son of Jesse, <u>a man after mine own heart, which shall fulfill all my will</u>"** (Acts 13: 22).

He called David a man after His own heart and a man who will faithfully represent Him. In other words, David will not do his own will but will faithfully do what God tells him to do in all things. This is called having integrity. It is one of the major reasons that a lot of people cannot move forward in ministry today; they are anointed but they lack integrity.

When you track your mentee's progress and you speak to your mentee concerning the areas that he or she is coming short, you should do it in love and not with a sense of criticism or a holier than thou attitude. Be always willing to challenge your mentee in love and tell him or her that developing integrity is vital if he or she wants to go anywhere with the Lord or be used by the Lord. God said in **Psalms 15:4** that He will have regards towards or bless the person that has the following attributes:

"...Who despises a vile man but honors those who fear the Lord, who keeps his oath even when it hurts" (NIV).

In other words, when such a person makes a promise, even if it costs him or her personal suffering, he or she will fulfill it; this is a person who has integrity. It is amazing how many people will bow out of a deal or an oath when they perceive the grass to be greener on the other side. This is one of the reasons why many marriages are in shambles today. Many people do not honor their words or promises anymore but God looks for a man or woman that keeps his or her word. For example, if Karen makes Jack an offer about something, Jack agrees to the offer and they seal the agreement and Karen will go away thinking that she has a solid deal with Jack. If however, Gina comes around and makes Jack a better offer and Jack immediately dumps Karen's offer without regards to the promise or agreement that he made with Karen, then we can conclude that Jack has no integrity. If this is consistently Jack's way of treating people, then God will have a hard time using Jack as His representative. He can still be anointed and praying for people but his ministry will not grow. God cannot place him on a national or international platform. This is what He said concerning people like Jack, "They will make me look bad. People will have a hard time trusting their God because they constantly demonstrate lack of integrity." It is true that if you are flip flopping and you go before people, they are going to think that you and your God are both flip floppers because that is what you demonstrate before them.

On the other hand, if you are a person who makes commitment and does not back out of a commitment just because another offer happens to benefit you better, God says that you are the type of person that He is looking for. When you fulfill your initial commitment and suffer loss because of a better offer that you turned down, God alone will make up the difference between what you lost in fulfilling that initial commitment and what you would have gained in the second one. What you lost becomes a sacrifice and God will honor and bless you for it.

One of the things that we see in the world today is selfishness. A lot of people live with the attitude of how can I get the most for the least effort? I am going to look for the people that can give me the most and I will fellowship with them and stick with them but I will stay away from people that are least profitable to me. This is not what God wants and it is not what He is raising us up to be. The Christian life is a sacrificial life.

Keys for Mentoring Women:

When it comes to mentoring women, a good guide is found in **Proverbs 31:10-31**:

> **"Who can find <u>a virtuous woman</u>? for <u>her price is far above rubies</u>. *11* <u>The heart of her husband doth safely trust in her</u>, so that <u>he shall have no need of spoil</u>. *12* <u>She will do him good and not evil</u> all the days of her life. *13* <u>She seeketh wool, and flax, and worketh willingly with her hands</u>. *14* She is like the merchants' ships; <u>she bringeth her food from afar</u>. *15* <u>She riseth also while it is yet night, and giveth meat to her household, and a portion to her maidens</u>. *16* <u>She considereth a field,</u>**

and buyeth it: with the fruit of her hands she planteth a vineyard. *17* She girdeth her loins with strength, and strengtheneth her arms. *18* She perceiveth that her merchandise is good: her candle goeth not out by night. *19* She layeth her hands to the spindle, and her hands hold the distaff. *20* She stretcheth out her hand to the poor; yea, she reacheth forth her hands to the needy. *21* She is not afraid of the snow for her household: for all her household are clothed with scarlet. *22* She maketh herself coverings of tapestry; her clothing is silk and purple. *23* Her husband is known in the gates, when he sitteth among the elders of the land. *24* She maketh fine linen, and selleth it; and delivereth girdles unto the merchant. *25* Strength and honour are her clothing; and she shall rejoice in time to come. *26* She openeth her mouth with wisdom; and in her tongue is the law of kindness. *27* She looketh well to the ways of her household, and eateth not the bread of idleness. *28* Her children arise up, and call her blessed; her husband also, and he praiseth her. *29* Many daughters have done virtuously, but thou excellest them all (*this is God's compliment to her*). *30* Favor is deceitful, and beauty is vain: but a

woman that feareth the LORD, she shall be praised. *31* **Give her of the fruit of her hands; and let her own works praise her in the gates.**"

From the above scripture, we can see that this woman is not an idle person. She does not make excuses but takes care of her household. She is willing to go out there and work and she is willing to rise up early and do what needs to be done. She is one who is willing to pull her weight and do what is needed to make her household run well or smoothly. Therefore, she does not have the attitude of some selfish people whose purpose in life is, "Me and my two or me and my husband are all I care about."

I watch the game show called *Deal or No Deal* and I would watch as the host of the show would ask the contestants what they would do with their winnings. It is shocking to watch the number of people who come on the show and all they think and care about are themselves. The question is usually in the line of, what would you do if you were to win a million dollars tonight? Some people had plans to do something for others or their communities besides themselves and their family members. There were some whose focus was just on themselves. They would reply saying, "Expand my house and build four bedrooms, pay off my debts, send my children to college" and the host would say, what more would you do with your winnings and the self focused contestants would reply, "Remodel the kitchen, go on vacation, maybe add another room, etc." The things they desire are not for others but for themselves and their nucleus family but not this woman in **Proverbs 31.** The woman in **Proverbs 31** is a very generous woman, she provides for her household, her servants, the poor and the needy. **She riseth also while it is yet night, and giveth meat to her household, and a portion to her maidens... She**

145

stretcheth out her hand to the poor; yea, she reacheth forth her hands to the needy.

She knows who she is in the Lord and as a result, does not have an identity issue. She is secured in who she is and therefore is not looking for a handout. **She seeketh wool, and flax, and worketh willingly with her hands. She considereth a field, and buyeth it: with the fruit of her hands she planteth a vineyard. She looketh well to the ways of her household, and eateth not the bread of idleness.** She is not waiting for a rich man to do everything for her. She is putting her hand to the spindle herself and getting things done. There are a lot of women who are looking for that good rich husband to do everything for them. What a lot of the women fail to realize is that the rich man is also looking for a woman who will not squander his money but has something to offer him as well. A rich man is not stupid; he does not want someone who would come into his life and then get rich off him and when she gets tired of him sue him for half of what he owns. This is why you see that the rich and famous usually marry amongst themselves because they do not want people that will come into their lives and walk off with half their wealth. This is what happens in rich families and in Hollywood. Do you see them marrying other people that are not like them?

This woman in **Proverbs 31** is not afraid to trade and she will do whatever it takes to bring help and resources into the house. When you look at verses 17 and 25, you will see that she has an inner strength and is not fearful about tomorrow—**she girdeth her loins with strength, and strengtheneth her arms...Strength and honour are her clothing; and she shall rejoice in time to come.** You can pretty much surmise that this woman knows who her God is and that her strength comes from the Lord. Therefore, she is not looking to herself but is looking at the strength that she gets from God and because of that, she is willing to do the things that others are waiting for people to come into their lives and do. In other words, she is not a Cinderella waiting for a Prince Charming to come and sweep her off her feet. She is not that kind of a person, if that happens, it will be a blessing to her but she is secure in who she is in her God. Her husband is pleased with her and her good works are known in the community. She sees a bright future for herself.

We get wisdom from the Word of the Lord so she knows scriptures and she speaks kindly to people. In other words, she knows how to talk to people because she is not rude but kind and generous. The law of kindness is in her tongue. Some ladies are beautiful until they open their months. They do not know how to address people and they do not know how to talk nicely to people; they are rude. They are like a book with a pretty book cover but contain very bad writing on the inside. You have probably come across some of them in your life experience and some men have taken some of these pretty books home only to be shocked at the very bad writing they contain. At the end, the men's attitude was, away, away with this bad book and the marriage ended in divorce.

By the same token, some women have taken home a guy that looked like he too was a very handsome book only to pay dearly by the verbal and physical abuse from a once good looking book and they too have gone away, away with this bad book. Therefore, let your beauty come from the inside. Have beauty of character, beauty of honesty and fidelity and beauty of kindness and love. These according to **Proverbs 31**, are more precious than rubies. In other words, God values these virtues more than gold and silver.

<u>**Note**</u>: *The following is an exercise for you and your mentee.*

Exercise: Measure Yourself on a Scale of 1-10

*When you are mentoring women, be sure to ask them during this exercise how they think they measure up to this woman in **Proverbs 31**. The question should be something like: On a scale of 1-10, how do you think you measure up to this woman that the scripture is talking about? In what areas do you see yourself coming short concerning the virtues that she displayed. This exercise will help you as the mentor to know where your mentee needs to be challenged and where he or she has the biggest struggles.*

*I believe that if you really break this down (analyze **Proverbs 31**) with your mentee during your one-on-one session, it will help you to see what your mentee thinks concerning employment, providing for one's family, interpersonal relationships, etc. It will help you to get a clear perception of who your mentee thinks she is. You can then show her that the **Proverbs 31** woman is secure in her identity and has no issues about work, charity and being kind to others. You can analyze each verse and use each verse as the measuring yardstick to rate your mentee or to have her rate herself. For example, the scripture says that "strength and honor are her clothing." You can then help your mentee to see how that the **Proverbs 31** woman honors herself and she does not go out there and present herself any which way or dress any which way. She is clothed with an inner strength and she honors herself by the way she dresses. According to verses 21 and 22, she is well attired—for **all her household are clothed with scarlet. She maketh herself coverings of tapestry; her clothing is silk and purple**. In other words, she does not dress like a "hoochie."*

I say to you that the materials in this book are quite effective because they actually help you to see how you can get a person to measure up on a scale.

Other Examples of
Virtuous Women in Scriptures

Abigail as a Virtuous and Wise Woman:

Besides, **Proverbs 31**, we also read in **1 Samuel 25:3** that there was a virtuous woman named Abigail. She was the wife of Nabal a very wicked man:

> **"Now the name of the man was Nabal; <u>and the name of his wife Abigail: and she was a woman of good understanding, and of a beautiful countenance:</u> but the man was churlish and evil in his doings; and he was of the house of Caleb."**

David was angry with Nabal because David sent his men to ask Nabal for food and Nabal refused to give them food for David and his men. Therefore, David vowed to destroy Nabal and his household but when Abigail (Nabal's wife) found out, she left in a hurry to meet David with food and other provisions. When David met Abigail, he was immediately captivated by her. One of the things that attracted David to Abigail was not just her beauty but her wisdom because she knew the Word of God that had been spoken over David and she reminded David about the promises of God upon his life. She used her wisdom to persuade David not to avenge himself with his own hands and she prophesied over David and she encouraged him concerning his situation with King Saul.

> **"...but I thine handmaid saw not the young men of my lord, whom thou didst send. *26* Now therefore, my lord, as the LORD liveth, and as thy soul liveth, <u>seeing</u>**

the LORD hath withholden thee from coming to shed blood, and from avenging thyself with thine own hand, now let thine enemies, and they that seek evil to my lord, be as Nabal. *27* And now this blessing which thine handmaid hath brought unto my lord, let it even be given unto the young men that follow my lord. *28* I pray thee, forgive the trespass of thine handmaid: for the LORD will certainly make my lord a sure house; because my lord fighteth the battles of the LORD, and evil hath not been found in thee all thy days. *29* Yet a man is risen to pursue thee, and to seek thy soul: but the soul of my lord shall be bound in the bundle of life with the LORD thy God; and the souls of thine enemies, them shall he sling out, as out of the middle of a sling. *30* And it shall come to pass, when the LORD shall have done to my lord according to all the good that he hath spoken concerning thee, and shall have appointed thee ruler over Israel; *31* That this shall be no grief unto thee, nor offence of heart unto my lord, either that thou hast shed blood causeless, or that my lord hath avenged himself: but when the

LORD shall have dealt well with my lord, then remember thine handmaid" (1 Samuel 25:25-31).

Abigail's wisdom and gracious words were so inspiring and assuring to David that he fell in love with her on the spot. As soon as David heard that her husband Nabal was dead, he said to himself, "I know who I want; that wise woman Abigail. Go get her for me" (paraphrased).

Esther as a Virtuous and Wise Woman:

A woman can make a memorable impression on a man by her virtuous ways and the wisdom that comes out of her mouth. I personally believe that it was what made the difference between Esther and all the other virgins in Babylon. Esther had learned virtuous ways and so much wisdom from her uncle Mordecai that it made a difference when she appeared before the king. Each virgin got to spend a night with the King Ahasuerus but when Esther came before the king, she had the Word of the Lord and the king probably heard so much wisdom coming out of this Jewish girl that he was shocked, intrigued and captivated. He was supposed to have been the one that is full of wisdom but I think that Esther surprised him with her godly wisdom.

A lot of people think that Esther was chosen because of her beauty but I do not think that it was all exterior or based solely on her looks. I believe that she said some things to the king that were straight out of scriptures and that were kingdom principles that became an eye opener to the king. I believe that the king liked what he heard, wanted to know more about this virtuous and wise girl and he wanted to hear from her again and again. If you really think about it, how many women can one man sleep with? I do not think it that it was all about the sex. I think it was about who the king wanted to spend time in a conversation with.

A lot of people do not challenge themselves to know the Word of the Lord but what they fail to realize is that it is in the Word of the Lord that you get true wisdom and it is in spending time with the Lord and His Word that you receive guidance from Him. As you spend time with Him and His Word, He gives you a panoramic view about life and His plan and purpose for you. He also begins to give you specific directions about even the small areas of your life. For example, there are times that I am spending time with the Lord in prayer and His Word and He would say to me, go clean your house or go clean your car. He knows that I do not like to wash my car by myself so He will usually give me a vision of my car on the highway with other cars and mine is the only one that is so dusty and needs to be washed. As much as I hate washing my car, I will get up and go hand wash my car. We have to be practical; we cannot be so spiritual that we do not touch the ground anymore. Therefore, help each one of your mentees to take a look at these scriptures in order to see where they really need to come up to the plate.

The Truth about Men:
One of the things that I have discovered in men is that some men would like to have a woman that does not have an opinion and does not know anything about anything but give them time and they will get bored with such woman. One of the reasons is because, when a man gets a woman that he can talk or relate to, there is a part of him that will come alive. God created us because He wanted a being in His own class that He can relate to and He set it up for us not to be alone but to have someone to fellowship with. A true man wants an intelligent woman and will feel frustrated when he tries

to have an intelligent conversation with someone who has nothing to offer back in that conversation. If you look at the scriptures account of life in heaven, you will notice that God has angels that worship Him and cry holy, holy all day and everyday. You will also see that He has Cherubims that bow down and fly around the throne and they too worship Him all day and every day but still, God wanted a being in His own class that He can have intelligent conversations with, so He created man. He wanted somebody to talk to and this is why He is exceptionally happy when we learn scriptures and their applications. He wants us to learn His ways and operate in them as He does. He made men the same way.

I know that I will personally get bored with someone who is immature and does not know scriptures and lacks intelligence. I will get bored with someone if I talk with him or her for more than five minutes and I do not see a level of development and maturity concerning life, scriptures and just plain common sense. I do not care how wealthy the person is because I like people with common sense. I will quickly get bored with someone who has nothing to offer in the area of wisdom. I believe that we all have to position ourselves in such a way that we have something to offer to the people that come into our lives. We can all bring something to the table. The **Proverbs 31** woman has a lot to offer and we can each look at her and see how she is willing to apply herself, how she relates to people, how she relates to her household, how she relates to the merchant people out there, her husband's perception of her and her children's perception of her. She is truly a woman in every sense of the word.

Abigail and Esther also had something to offer when they met their husbands. They had something to offer to those that came in contact with them. They were wise and virtuous women and we all can learn from them.

<u>*Note:*</u> *For a more detailed discussion of the* **Proverbs 31** *woman, see my other book titled,* **Looking for a Perfect Mate? Qualities of a Godly Man and Woman.**

Keys for Mentoring Men:

We are now going to address how to mentor the men in a way that is unique to them. The Apostle Paul's letters to Timothy (I and II Timothy) and other scriptures in the New Testament are very good guides for mentoring men. For example, Paul instructs Timothy about how he is to conduct himself and how he should deal with different people. The mentor should use the scriptures that I am about to discuss as a measuring scale just as we used **Proverbs 31** with the women. Ask your male mentees how they think they measure up to the qualities that we are about to discuss and also ask them the areas that they need your assistance as you discuss them. Therefore, the mentor should tell the mentee to realistically evaluate himself to see how he compares to this man called Timothy.

Paul tells us in **1 Timothy 1:5** that all the commandments are summed up in one word—love! This love must come out of a pure heart, a good conscious and sincere faith.

> **"Now the end of the commandment is charity out of <u>a pure heart</u>, and of <u>a good conscience</u>, and of <u>faith unfeigned</u>."**

As a true man of God, your heart must be pure and you must have a good conscience. Also, your faith must be sincere. This means that you do not just say what sounds good to people, but what is true and what is sincere. Do not be like the politicians that come out and tell the people what they think the people need to hear in order to get their votes and after that forget all their promises. To them, the people do not count anymore until the next election.

In **1 Timothy 3:1-2,** Paul outlines the qualities of a bishop and a deacon. The truth of the matter is that the qualities that a bishop and a deacon are being exhorted to have, every single Christian man should also have. Every man of God that wants a successful Christian walk must possess these same qualities:

> **"This is a true saying, If a man desire the office of a bishop, he desireth a good work. <u>2 A bishop then must be blameless</u>, the <u>husband of one wife</u>, <u>vigilant</u>, <u>sober</u>, <u>of good behaviour</u>, <u>given to hospitality</u>, <u>apt to teach</u>;"**

You are to be blameless. Being blameless means that you should not to be found guilty of evil deeds and you should not give occasion for people to reproach the name of Christ. There should not be a brawl and you, the man of God are right in the middle of it. You must avoid the appearance of evil. You are to be committed to one woman—your wife! You are to be faithful to your spouse. This means that as a married man, you should not have a girlfriend out there and still continue to say that you only have one wife. When you examine scriptures closely, you will see that God defines marriage by a sexual union. If you sleep with a lady, you become one with her in that sexual union.

One of the revelations about why God only permitts divorce on the grounds of adultery was because when a man or a woman engages in a sexual union with someone that is not his or her spouse, he or she actually sets his or her marriage aside (divorces his or her spouse) spiritually by the act. Therefore, the Lord allows divorce on the grounds of adultery because the marriage has already been set aside spiritually. In other words, the adulterous spouse has already spiritually divorced his or her spouse by the act of adultery. Being faithful to your spouse is therefore a very serious matter. This is the reason why a spouse that has spiritual discernment can tell when his or her marriage partner has been unfaithful because when the spouse comes home from an adulterous situation, the spiritually discerning spouse can tell that the spiritual atmosphere in the home has changed because another spirit is now united with the spouse that had been unfaithful.

All men of God are exhorted by the above scripture to be vigilant, to be sober, to be of good behavior and to be given to hospitality. As a man of God, you are to be spiritually alert and sensitive when things are not right or when an atmosphere is not right for you. You should not be temperamental or quick tempered but should model good behavior. Some men are very hostile to people and especially to women. You should practice walking in love. Do not use the fact that you are a man to keep you from expressing love to your spouse, sons, daughters and others. We are to be known for our "love walk." It also means that you as a man of God must walk in forgiveness. Learn to forgive those that have done you wrong and do not walk in revenge. Do not beat up your spouse or other people but learn self restraint.

A true man of God will provide for his family. Do not neglect your responsibilities as a son, a husband and a father. Be a good provider. According to **1 Timothy 5:8**, a man who does not provide for his family has denied his Christian faith (no longer a Christian) and he is worst than unbelievers:

"But <u>if any provide not for his own, and specially for those of his own house, he hath denied the faith,</u> and <u>is worse than an infidel</u> *(an unbeliever)."*

Also, a true man of God will not only be a good provider but will not abandon his family and seek greener pastures only for himself. Being the head of the family and being the provider for your family is a God-given assignment to all men and He will hold them accountable for their conducts at the end.

Also, you as the true man of God are to have good business ethics and work habits. This means that you cannot be slothful, lazy, idle and unreliable and expect God to bless you and the work of your hands. If you look around today, a lot of men have become drifters. They move away from their families, walk away from jobs and are living like vagabonds. They have no commitment to anything and they are full of excuses as to why their lives are in a sorry state. Therefore, I exhort the man of God to be faithful, committed and diligent at his work. Be a good role model for all who see you or come in contact with you. Be a faithful witness for Christ everywhere you go.

Do not be prideful regardless of your accomplishments. God hates pride and He will wrestle with any man who is prideful. He will not grant His grace to those that are proud but to those that are humble. We see this in **James 4:6**:

"...God resisteth the proud, but <u>giveth grace unto the humble</u>."

Therefore, in order for you to receive God's grace, stay away from pride and walk humbly towards all that you meet or deal with. Let others sing your praise and do not toot your own horn. Pride stinks. A true man of God is to follow after righteousness, godliness, faith, love, patience, meekness and to fight the good fight of faith.

According to **1 Timothy 3:3**, a man of God should not be a drunk or a covetous person. Alcohol abuse can make a complete fool of a man or woman who abuses it. It leads to ungodly and unruly behaviors. Being covetous can also drive a man to ungodly compromise and to do ungodly things.

> **"Not given to wine, no striker, not greedy of filthy lucre; but patient, not a brawler, not covetous;"**

Avoid greed and do not fall into the love of money. Instead, be a man that is led by the Holy Spirit in all that you do. Let the love of God always be your motivating factor. In other words, the love for God and the love for people should be the reason for the things you do.

Also, Paul tells Timothy that as a man of God, he should avoid some things and to walk in righteousness. For instance, he told Timothy not to rebuke an elder publicly and that there should be two or three witnesses when he is presiding over a case. He tells Timothy to honor widows. Paul also tells him that he should not allowed people to despise him because of his youth and he even tells him how he is to take care of himself because of his physical ailment. Paul further tells Timothy how to instruct the people who will help continue to teach others so that the Gospel can be carried forth.

> **"But thou, O man of God, flee these things; and follow after righteousness, godliness, faith, love, patience, meekness"** (1 Timothy 6:11).

Also, Timothy is supposed to stir up the gifts of God within him and he is supposed to treat the elders with respect and the younger ones in love. He is supposed to make sure that the doctrines in the church are sound doctrines. This means that the man of God must not accept doctrines that are contrary to biblical doctrines. He should not allow himself to be polluted by people that are preaching different types of doctrines. He is supposed to hold on to those good things that Paul has taught him as his mentor.

Timothy was also to stay away from profane and vain babblings. He is to stay away from those scientific studies that are in opposition to the Word of God. As it is stated above, he is to walk in **righteousness, godliness, faith, love, patience, meekness and to fight the good fight of faith. He is to "lay hold on eternal life, whereunto thou art also called, and hast professed a good profession before many witnesses."** A true man of God should therefore have an eternal perspective on life and walk in righteousness before all that observe him.

Paul gives Timothy a very serious charge before God the Father and the Lord Jesus Christ in **1 Timothy 6:13-14**:

> **"I give thee charge in the sight of God, who quickeneth all things, and before Christ Jesus, who before Pontius Pilate witnessed a good confession; *14* That thou keep this commandment without spot, unrebukeable, until the appearing of our Lord Jesus Christ:"**

In other words, Timothy is supposed to behave well, follow after the things that are good and godly and to be patient with all people and exercise meekness and love. He is not to do anything that will give occasion for someone to say to him, you knew better not to have done that. Do not give occasion for people to rebuke you for something you knew to avoid doing. This is also the standard that our men are being called and challenged to uphold because God is no respecter of persons. If He gave this scripture to Paul to give to Timothy, it is also for the men of today and for us women too.

What happens today is that people do the ungodly things that they desire to do with the plan to repent afterwards. As I stated before, ministry is by reputation. A great deal of your ministry is based on your good reputation. If you ruin your good reputation, you may damn your ministry because if the word out there is that you are a fornicator, you are unreliable, you have no integrity and you are dishonest, who do you think is going to want to come sit under your ministry? Many men have ruined their ministries by ruining their good reputation and once you ruin your good reputation, it is hard to get it back.

That is why when you look at somebody like the Prophet Daniel in the book of Daniel Chapter 4, you will see where his jealous colleagues set out to find fault with him. This is a very good scripture on the importance of honesty and integrity because first, they looked at Daniel's personal life. If you look at the way that the scripture is rendered, you will notice that it says that <u>they tried to find fault in his work</u> but they could not. Next, <u>they tried to find fault in his character</u> but they could not and they tried <u>others areas of Daniel's life for faults</u> but they could not find any fault in Daniel so the only way they could find fault with Daniel was to make an ungodly or pagan law and to get the king to sign it into effect. The one and only reason they did this was because they knew that Daniel was very faithful and dedicated to the worship of his God and that he would never agree to worship a man or an idol. They saw this as Daniel's weakness. How many of us can stand the test of such an intense and close scrutiny? What will people find if they look into your personal life as a man of God? Would you be found to be a faithful and true man of God or will the result come out that you are a hypocrite? When no one is watching you, do you do what you say in the public?

We know that the persecution ended with Daniel being vindicated by God when He sent an angel to shut the mouths of the lions and we know that the king avenged Daniel by killing all the people that had plotted destruction against him. God will always protect a man who demonstrates integrity before Him. Therefore, the men of God should not have to compromise their Christian faith for anything even if their lives are at stake.

The mentor should work closely with the mentee to make sure that he understands the importance of all the above attributes that we have discussed. According to the Apostle Paul, you will not be unfruitful or barren if you possess these attributes.

> **"For if these things be in you, and abound, they make you that ye shall neither be barren nor unfruitful in the knowledge of our Lord Jesus Christ"** (2 Peter 1:8).

It is possible to let those things that have been given to you slip through neglect. As the mentor, exhort your mentee not to let the gifts of God and the Word of God spoken over him or her slip. Exhort your mentee to learn to be a man of prayer and to learn to war with the Word that God was spoken over him.

Dr. Mary J. Ogenaarekhua

"This charge I commit unto thee, son Timothy, according to the prophecies which went before on thee, that thou by them mightest war a good warfare" (1 Timothy 1:18).

I believe that the mentor and the mentee will both benefit from the exercise of using these scriptures above as a measuring scale for the male mentees.

Other Examples of Godly Men in Scriptures

The Life of Joseph in Genesis:

Also Joseph is a good example of a godly man to study with your mentee. Encourage your mentee to look at the life of Joseph. He will see how Joseph was initially immature and got himself into a place where his brothers tried to kill him but even in the midst of all his troubles he was able to grow. As you observe his different stages of development and preparation for what God had for him, you will see how he maintained his integrity. He did not blame his situation on being in prison and being framed wrongly for a crime that he did not commit. There is not an account of Joseph blaming anybody. In fact, he wept over his brothers that had sold him into slavery because he loved them.

It takes a man of God to look at his wicked brothers in love, to hug them and to weep over them. Only a man that God has taught His ways can do this type of thing. When his brothers were afraid for their lives because of what they had done to him, Joseph addressed them in love and assured them that it was not them that sent him to Egypt but God in order that he could prepare a place for them to be nourished so that they did not starve! He did not hold their wickedness towards him over their heads and seek revenge against them.

Therefore, as a man of God, you have to challenge yourself to make the best out of life and not blame your dad and others for not being there for you when you were young. Do not couch on your past and use it as an excuse not to be a man today, an excuse for not providing for your family and an excuse to remain a failure in life.

I have spoken to several men who told me that they did not go to college because they were just so "sure that even if they went to college, they would not get a job." They claim that "the man" would not give them a job even if they had a college education. It is happening in the black community. I have come down hard on some of them by asking them, "Who told you that you would not have been an exception even if it was the case that a lot of educated black males do not have job? Who told you that you could not have been an exception?" It is sad for people to defeat themselves before they even try. **I believe the saying that "the worst failure is the failure to try" because you eliminate yourself all together from even being a candidate.** I say to the men, especially the black men, do not disqualify yourself no matter what because with God, all things are possible. He can make a way for you where there is no way.

Moses and Joshua/Elijah and Elisha:

If you look at the relationship that was between Moses and Joshua, and Elijah and Elisha, you can see how Moses worked with Joshua. Joshua was very faithful to Moses and stayed with Moses till the end of Moses' life. It was the same way that Elisha was faithful to Elijah until Elijah was caught up by God into heaven. Both Moses and Elijah used the relationship that they had with their pupils (Joshua and Elisha) as a training, mentoring and discipleship tool. Therefore, when you are working with men to help develop them into godly men, you have to tell them about the dynamics of the relationships between Moses and Joshua and Elijah and Elisha. They can learn from their commitment, from their dedication, and from their loyalty and honesty. Neither Joshua nor Elisha used their past as excuses to keep from performing their duties to God and to their earthly masters or leaders.

Today, we have women heading up households and this is not the way that God intended for it to be. A lot of men have abandoned their God-assigned roles as the head of their household and others have just simply relinquished their duties to the women. There is a cry in the body of Christ and in society at large for men to rise up and take back their positions as sons, husbands, fathers and priests of their homes as God intended for them to.

Even in the church, some men go to church not because they are committed to God or truly interested in their Christian growth but just to get their wives off their backs. This is sad because I know a lot of women who have to prod and preach to their husbands to pray or go to church. A lot of men do not read their Bibles and the result is that the devil comes into their lives and dislocates them from their homes, their jobs and from their church. These are some of the things that the mentor needs to stress to the mentee to avoid. The Word of God still remains that we are to seek God's kingdom first:

> **"But seek ye first the kingdom of God, and his righteousness; and all these things shall be added unto you"** (Matthew 6:33).

All men need to know that God's kingdom should come first. When they do this, God will give them that which they desire. Their human efforts can only carry them so far but God supplies all needs.

A Look at Titus:

Do a study of the life of Titus as he walked with Paul in his missionary journeys and see the integrity that he demonstrated as a man of God. As the mentor, you have to make sure that you challenge your male mentees to come to that place where they can look and see a standard of what they are being called to become. Sometimes, people do not know what they are supposed to be doing but when God uses you as the mentor to lay it out for them in the Bible, they can get a visual of what God is saying. Therefore, if necessary, do a mini-Bible study on these scriptures about the men of God that we have discussed above.

Again, I say that God has a standard; God is looking for that man or that woman that is in His image and after His character or likeness. Let the men know that this means that God is looking for the person that will faithfully demonstrate His character and His integrity. It is unfortunate that a lot of us want to be prepared for ministry but we do not prepare ourselves as honest and righteous people. Many do not think that building character and building integrity is part of preparation for ministry but what they do not know is that these are the things God looks for in a person before He launches the person into ministry.

Summary:

In summary, I say to the mentor that when you realistically analyze your mentee with all the above scriptures, you will clearly be able to see where he or she is as a true man or woman of God. Again, use the scriptures in Proverbs 31, Abigail in 1 Samuel, Esther, 1 and 11 Timothy, Titus, Moses and Joshua, Joseph, Elijah and Elisha and also the Prophet Daniel. They will help you to see where your mentee needs your help. As I stated before, do not try to be all-in-all to your mentee. Instead, recognize where he or she needs professional help and be willing to steer him or her to a Christian professional in that area. That means that you have to be willing to steer them to a trained counselor if he or she needs a trained counselor. If your mentee needs to be grounded in sound biblical truths or just know the Word of God, you have to be willing to send him or her to where there is a sound Bible study. The key is to recognize when your mentee needs the type of help that is beyond your level, training or skills and be willing to help him or her get it. It does not diminish your ability as a mentor but rather, it shows that you are mature and secure in who you are and in what God has called you to do.

Basically, you should always try to caution yourself not to take on more than you can handle because if you do, you can get overwhelm by the whole thing. I also said in the beginning that if you feel like you got into a mentoring relationship without truly hearing from the Lord first but you thought you did, that you should do as I do, run to the Lord to get you out of it. I am one that always runs to the Lord when I am in a tight situation and I cry out to Him to get me out. If what you were doing is not what He has for you, He will find a way to get you out of it.

Resources:
The primary resource material for the mentor and the mentee is the Holy Bible. The Word of God is the best thing on planet earth and nothing compares with it. Everyone should have a copy of the Bible as well as a good Study Bible.

I said in the beginning that both the mentor and the mentee need to find materials on mentoring that will help them to better understand what mentoring is and what mentoring is not. My workbook on mentoring titled, *A Workbook for Successful Mentoring* is very helpful. I advice you to get a copy because it contains actual lessons for each step of the mentoring process.

Also, the book titled, *Guardians of the Gate: Enriching Your Life Through Spiritual Mentoring* by Ann Platz is very insightful concerning mentoring. You might want to also have it in your collection because it is a good book. It tells you about the different types of mentoring and how you can mentor someone for a short time and you are given grace for that time or you can mentor someone for a month or a year. Everyone needs to know that all mentoring relationships are not long term.

I always recommend Watchman Nee's *"Spiritual Authority"* to all my students and to all my mentees. I strongly recommend that you read this book because it is really good on authority. The reason that I strongly recommend it is because no matter what you do or where you go, if you do not recognize authority, it will only be a question of time before you disobey your assigned authority or come across to others as rude, obnoxious or rebellious. When you disobey the godly authority over you, you open yourself up to spiritual attacks by rebellious spirits that you invited when you disregarded or disrespected the spiritual authority over you. It is good to make sure you have a good understanding of authority both inside and outside of the church because when you go against the devil, you want to make sure that there is no rebellion in your own life. I said on *page 211* of one of my books titled, *"How to Discern and Expel Evil Spirits"* that anyone who is in rebellion cannot cast out any rebellious spirits. The truth of the matter is, when you ask the Lord to release you to go after the devil and his evil spirits, you are asking to go after rebellious spirits. Therefore, there must be no rebellion in you against God or against His authority.

You are to go after rebellious spirits after your obedience is complete. We see this in **2 Corinthians 10:6**:

> **"...And having in a <u>readiness to revenge all disobedience, when your obedience is fulfilled</u>."**

From the above scripture, you can clearly see why you do not need to be in disobedience to God's Word or authority when you go after evil spirits. All authority belongs to God but we have those who misuse their authority and God will judge them. The Bible says in **Romans 14:10** that, **"we shall all stand before the Judgment Seat of Christ."**

I know I covered a little bit more in this chapter because it is really the core of what you do concerning your mentee and it outlines what is being required of the mentee. Therefore, I had to spend a bit more time in it.

<u>Note</u>: Remember that these materials were first presented in actual classroom settings.

Question and Answer Session

Cindy: My question is on confidentiality. Does the mentee have to be confidential as well as the mentor?

Mary: Yes, there is a need for confidentiality because if you come and share your personal business with me, I am not going to go around and blab to everybody or even to another person. It is the same way that every mentor should behave because you do not want your personal business put out there. I would think that confidentiality works both ways. It is just like going to see a doctor; you do not go out there and broadcast your personal health issues and neither does your doctor. I would think that it would be in the best interest of both the mentor and the mentee to keep their business private unless it is a testimony that they both wish to share with the public or a special group of people. If you want your mentor to share your specific situation with others, you can tell your mentor about it and you can let him or her know that you want to share it as a testimony or that you want him or her to feel free to share it. Anytime you are going to say something that involves another person and you are using the person's name, you have to get the person's permission because we are living in a society that is so replete with law suites and you do not want to get sued. Therefore, be careful not to put yourself in a position that someone can sue you and tarnish your name because as I said earlier, ministry is by reputation. You want to have a good reputation.

Karen: How about the area of prayer; you said don't lay hands on a person unless you ask the person's permission. Well, as for prayer, I am thinking maybe I can ask the person, would you like to pray about this? In other words, I am giving them an opportunity to say, "Yes, I would like to" or "No, I don't want to."

Mary: If the person is sitting right in front of you, you have to ask the person for permission because if the person does not want to pray, you will then know to leave the person alone. But the Bible does tell us **to pray for all men and make supplications to the Lord concerning government.**

> **"I exhort therefore, that, first of all, supplications, prayers, intercessions, and giving of thanks, be made for all men;**
> **2 For kings, and for all that are in authority; that we may lead a quiet and peaceable life in all**

godliness and honesty. *3* For this is good and acceptable in the sight of God our Saviour; *4* <u>Who will have all men to be saved, and to come unto the knowledge of the truth</u>..." (1Timothy 2:1-4).

The saints (all believers) are mandated by the Word of God to pray for everybody. Therefore, we can pray for all men during our personal prayer times. For example, I can pray for the President of this country and I can pray for everyone in this country during my personal prayer time. I do not have to write to the President to get his permission to pray for him nor do I have to get the permission of everyone in this country before I can pray for them. It is a different scenario when you are with someone face to face and you want to pray for the person. It will be rude to start calling the person's name in their presence as you are praying. It is the courteous thing to do by asking the person's permission when you are face to face with the person

Also, if you told someone that you have been praying for them and they do not want you to pray for them, leave them alone and go to the Lord with the situation. I will go to the Lord because I had a situation some years ago in which someone confronted me because the person was so "sure" that I had been praying for them because the person was not a Christian. After telling the person that they were not that important, I also told them that the Bible says to pray for the salvation of all men. It is their choice whether or not they want to be Christian. I told the person that Jesus does not force Himself on anyone.

Gina: How about speaking peace to a place before you enter the place? I know the question is not related to what we are saying but could you speak to that anyway?

Mary: I will answer it because other people can learn from the answer. I also had an incident with someone about speaking peace to a place before you enter the place. As for me, I take the Lord's commandments seriously and **one of the things that He commanded us to do when we go to a place is say, "Peace" to the place.** Therefore, I try to be diligent in saying peace to every place that I go to in obedience to the Lord's command. Moreover, I do not want to walk into anyone's spiritual chaos, unrest and ungodly spiritual atmosphere. It gives me and hopefully the people in the place peace while I am there. The following is the incident that happened as a result of my speaking peace to a place.

One day, I was invited to meet a new neighbor who had just moved into my apartment complex and because I am so used to speaking peace to places, I must have softly said peace to the place in Jesus name before I entered the apartment. He never said anything to me but he was offended and angry with me for it and I was not aware of how he felt but every once in a while, I would see a vision of this neighbor trying to engage me in a fight.

One Sunday morning, as I came out to get in my car to go to church, he ran out to confront me. Mind you, this was after one year. He proceeded to say some foolish things and finally he got to the root of his anger. He said, "When you were invited to my apartment, you spoke peace and the name of Jesus into my apartment and I did not give you permission to do so because Jesus is not my Lord." I tried to ask him if he was allergic to peace but when I saw the spirit that I was dealing with in him, I said, "Jesus said to me that everyplace I go to, I should say peace to the place. Therefore, I was obeying Jesus and you may not have made Him your Lord, but He is my Lord and He is Lord of all." When he tried to counter what I said, I quoted the scripture that said, "The earth is the Lord's and the fullness thereof" and I declared to the spirit that Jesus was higher than him. He insisted that he did not give me permission to speak peace and the name of Jesus into his apartment. I said again to him that Jesus is Lord of all and that the Lord Jesus' commandment was higher than his permission. I was amazed at what came out of his mouth next. He said, "Yes, Jesus is Lord of all, but he is not my Lord." I found out later that he belonged to a cult and that it was divine wisdom that led me to speak peace in Jesus name before entering his apartment.

I have learned not to speak so loud for people to hear when I speak peace to a place. I use wisdom but I still say peace because one of the things that it does is bless the people who are in the place (if they are worthy of it), it removes chaos from my path, it removes disaster from my path and it keeps me from partaking of the negative effects of other people's sins in the place. God does not want us to step into some kind of chaos or the evil things that are at work in the places we go. When you speak peace to a place before you go into it, you disarm any spiritual unrest in the place and you disarm any demonic uprising in the place. I believe that every Christian should speak peace to everywhere they go because our word of peace will produce stillness in the atmosphere spiritually while we are there and when we leave, they might resume their craziness spiritually but at least while we are there, we want peace. It will also help us tremendously when we visit our unsaved relatives.

According to the Lord, when we speak peace to a place, and because peace is a spirit, it will search all the people in the place to see if there is anyone that is worthy for it to rest on. It will only rest on the person that is worthy of peace because the scriptures say in **Isaiah 57:21** that **"there is no peace to the wicked."** Therefore, if peace cannot find anyone that is worthy for it to rest on, it will come back to you! You will have peace regardless.

> **"And into whatsoever house ye enter, first say, Peace be to this house. 6 And if the son of peace be there, your peace shall rest upon it: if not, it shall turn to you again"** (Luke 10:5-6).

Therefore, speak peace because even when the people in the place are not worthy of peace, you will have peace while you are there. It is a weapon.

Also, the Lord said that we should not enter into a strongman's house unless we first bind up the strongman. Your peace will actually take authority over the strongman in the places you go to. You can see the Lord Jesus' demonstration of this when He rebuked the raging wind by saying, **"Peace, be still!"** in **Mark 4:39**. The winds were raging out of control and all He said to restore calmness was, **"Peace, be still."** A lot of Christians get afflicted in places they go to because they do not take authority over the strongman in those places. They just walk into people's houses and they do not know what the people in those houses worshiped, what has been set up in those houses that attracts demons and what evil has been said or done in the houses.

Maybe someone was killed and they may think that they have thoroughly wiped away the person's blood, but the blood is still in the house speaking vengeance.

I thank God that I always speak peace to the places that I go to because an Asian lady once invited me to her apartment to pray for her because her spouse had walked out on her. I spoke peace before entering but I was amazed at how oppressed the apartment was. She was a baby Christian so I asked the Lord what the oppression was and He said that she still had books and other items from her previous religion in the apartment. He told me to ask her permission to see her bedroom and I did.

When I stepped into it, I was amazed at what she had done to the walls in her bedroom. She had them covered with nude pictures of her husband. I told her that the pictures have to come down as well as the books and other items from her past before we can pray. Such a setting would have been bad for a Christian who is struggling with pornography. If an undiscerning Christian were to walk into her living room, he or she might leave the apartment with the spirit of pornography in the place trying to enter or reenter his or her life. They did not have to go into the bedroom because the spirit was given free expression in the apartment.

Therefore, I advice you to speak peace to everywhere you go. You do not want the devil trying to attach things to you in the places that you go. Now, this does not mean that you can speak peace to a place such as a strip club and then sit down to watch the naked men or women dance. You will leave that place with those spirits attached to you because you fellowshipped with them.

Chapter 6

Avoiding the Pitfalls of Mentoring

There are some mistakes that are commonly made by some people as they come together in a relationship or as they interact one with another. These are what we call pitfalls and our goal is to avoid them in our mentoring relationships. I am going to outline them in a bullet point format so be sure to read them carefully and pay attention to them during your mentoring relationships so that you and your mentee will end your mentoring relationship on a good note. Let the end of your mentoring relationship bring praise and glory to the Lord's name.

I want you to know that a lot of people make these mistakes but I am hoping that after you have read about them below, you are going to safeguard yourself so that you do not make the same mistakes.

- **Let the Mentor/Mentee See the Real You:**
  The first point that I would like to make is that you should let your mentor see the real you. Also, to the mentor I say, let your mentee see the real you. Do not put on what we call the Sunday face and pretend to be who you are not. If you are putting on a different personality, a different character and a different face and someone is supposed to be helping you, the person is not going to be able to help you because you are not really presenting to them who you truly are. In order for your mentor to get to know you, he or she needs to see the real you; he or she needs to know where you are weak and where you are strong so they can effectively

175

plan how to help you. People get disappointed in a person when they discover that the person has been pretending to be who he or she is really not. Therefore, do not try to prove anything to your mentor; just be real with him or her. My counsel is for both the mentor and mentee to be real with each other.

- **Your Mentor/Mentee Should not Replace God, Your Spouse, Your Children, Your Friends, etc:** You cannot neglect your primary relationships in the name of mentoring another person or because of your mentor. Also, your mentee or mentor should not replace your spouse, your children and your friends. In other words, keep your primary relationships primary. Do not schedule things with your mentee knowing that it is your family that is always having to sacrifice. Honor your spouse, your children and your friends with your time.

Do not try to be God to your mentee and the mentee should not let the mentor replace God in his or her life. If you let your mentor/mentee relationship replace God or replace your spouse, your children or your friends, you are setting yourself up for a great battle down the road because, one, God is going to be very displeased with you and so will your spouse and your children. You will have warfare at home because the children want their mother or father, your spouse needs you and you cannot abandon your friends just because you have a person that is looking up to you for mentoring. You cannot neglect the important people in your life, so make sure that you maintain your primary relationships.

I have discovered that you have to work at relationships in order for them to be successful. I liken interpersonal relationship to a burning fire; if you leave it alone, the flame will quench and it will burn down. The ambers will just die out but if you fan the flames of your interpersonal relationship, it will continue to grow and its flame will increase. It takes work to make your relationships successful so do not neglect them or abandon them because of your mentoring relationship. Besides your immediate family, reach out to your friends and your extended family members so that they do not feel unloved and unwanted. I do not believe the saying that, "absence makes the heart grow fonder." People will forget you when they think you no longer want them in your life. This is why the Bible says in **Proverbs 18:24** that **"A man that hath friends must shew himself friendly..."** So keep your friends and keep your family. Your relationship with God is primary and anything that replaces God in your life is not to be encouraged.

Do not make idols of people and do not let others idolize you. I said in one of the previous chapters that I had a nightly prayer that I usually pray and I have now included in my prayer book titled, *Effective Prayer for Various Situations (Volume 1)*. They are, *the cleansing prayers* and they are very powerful prayers and I wanted everyone that I knew to pray them in order to cleanse themselves. Before the prayer book was published, I used to make copies and hand them out to people and I encouraged people to give copies to their relatives and friends. I wanted everyone to protect themselves from any spiritual assignments or attacks that had been sent against them. As it turned out, people began to praise me instead of praising the Lord. I cried out to the Lord to deliver me because it was idolatry and He corrected and delivered me. I learned not to let anybody replace God or give to me the glory that belongs to the Lord. Make sure that God has His proper position and place in your life and in the life of the mentee.

- **Your Mentor is Not Your Counselor Unless He or She is Trained:**
  I have said it before in the previous chapters but I say it again because we are talking about pitfalls: Your mentor is not your counselor unless he or she has been trained. Do not depend on your mentor to help you with deep emotional wounds because she or he may not be trained in this area. Therefore, both the mentor and mentee cannot take on more than they can handle when it comes to counseling. This is a good warning. Refer to Question and Answer Session in Chapter 4 for a detailed discussion of this. If you know that you are not a trained counselor, do not let them call you and lie on your couch and speak for hours and take up your time on a daily basis. It does not mean that you will not listen to someone that has problems. It means that you do not want them to back into you into the position of a counselor that you have not been trained to operate in. If you begin to operate as the counselor in their lives, you cannot refer them to where they can receive professional Christian counseling and by doing this you will essentially hinder their spiritual growth.

- **Your Mentor is Not Your Pastor:**
  Do not let your mentor replace your pastor when you know that you have a real pastor unless you are being mentored by your pastor in which case, your mentor is your pastor. Some people use their mentors to replace their pastor and this is wrong unless again, your pastor is also your mentor. Therefore, as a mentor, do not begin to operate as the pastor in your mentee's life. There are times that you might need to refer your mentee to his or her pastor. One time, I had to tell a lady, "You know what? I am not your pastor. Don't you have a pastor?" She said, "I do" and I said, "You need to go tell these problems to your pastor and see if the church has programs setup to help you in this area because this is the time for you to speak to your pastor." Depending on your financial status, you as the mentor cannot help someone to get or move out of an apartment and you cannot help someone to relocate but a pastor can. This is why the mentor has to be realistic and recognize when it is a problem that the church might have a solution for; such as a benevolence fund and they can help the person where you cannot. Be willing to steer your mentee to his or her pastor when needed.

- **Your Mentoring Sessions Should not Replace Your Membership in a Church or Your Church Attendance:**
  I once had a lady come to my office and I was talking to her and I wanted to know where she was fellowshipping; what church affiliation she had and she was like, "Oh no, I don't get involved like that anymore because (she called the name of her mentor) that's who I see now." I said, "So you don't go to church anymore?" She said that the mentor has

179

replaced her going to church and I proceeded to ask her how often she sees the mentor and she said every two or three months. What I came away with in the conversation was that this person was not in church. I told her that the mentor should not replace her pastor or her church membership. As Christians, we are to have one-on-one as well as corporate fellowship and there is a corporate anointing that we all need to partake of and be a part of in a church service. God's Word says in **Psalms 133:1** that it is beautiful and good when brethren are together in unity.

We are built for relationships, God said it Himself in Genesis that it is not good for man to be alone and not just in the marital setting but in life as a whole. Scientific studies have shown that people who are alone tend to have more health issues than people who are in relationships. When a person is alone, he or she has no one to talk to, no one to share his or her joy with and in times of sorrow or grief, the person can easily slip into depression. God wants you to have a physical person that you are in a relationship with and He wants you to be a part of His church family. It is not healthy for someone not to be part of a church when the person is born again and Spirit-filled. Therefore, you should not neglect your church family because of your mentoring relationship. Demonstrate your faithfulness and your integrity to the Lord by committing to do something in the house of the Lord and follow through because you have to sow in order to reap. Be a member of a church and keep up your church attendance.

- **Have a Kingdom Perspective Concerning Your Mentoring Relationship:**
  Do not use worldly counsel that contradicts the

Word of God; in other words, do not lay aside sound biblical principles in order to run to a quick fix that the world offers. Always have the perspective that your mentoring relationship is something that you are doing to bring praise and glory to the Lord and also to advance His kingdom. Therefore, do not engage in or encourage things that will not advance the kingdom or things that will bring reproach to the Lord. God the Father taught me a long time ago that "the end does not justify the means." He cares about what we do, why we do what we do and how we accomplish it all.

- **Do Not Date Your Mentor or Mentee:**
  The relationship between the mentor and the mentee should be treated as a professional relationship, so do not date your mentee. Do not get into a sexual relationship with your mentor or your mentee and if the mentee is looking up to you as his or her mentor, do not take advantage of their fascination or attraction to you. It is just like when a student has a crush on his or her teacher; do not take advantage of your mentee's vulnerability. If it actually gets to that point, one of the things you need to do is bring a third party into the equation. Let a third party deal with the mentee but explain to the mentee that you think that another person is more suitable to continue the mentoring but do not make the mentee to feel ashamed or ridiculed.

- **Always Pray Concerning Your Mentoring Sessions:**
  In other words, when you come together always commit your mentoring sessions to the Lord because this will help you to always bring the Lord

into perspective as the head of your mentoring relationship. I keep a kingdom perspective by making sure that I pray with my mentee for us to both receive instructions from the Lord. Therefore, always begin your sessions with prayer and a focus on God. This is also the way that you and your mentee can give God His proper position in your relationship. Do not let your mentee make you his or her God. Therefore, praying with him or her will ensure that they learn on their own to look up to God for answers. God and not you is the source of all answers.

- **Allow God's Word to be the Final Say So in All Your Decisions:**
  In other words, if you and your mentee decide to do something or take a course of action, you have to make sure it is biblical. For instance, as I stated in a previous chapter, if you are mentoring someone and you discover that the mentee has a limited knowledge of Word of God, you have to discuss that with the mentee. The two of you will have to come to a decision that yes, the mentee needs to attend a Bible study some place. You let the mentee know that it is in his or her best interest to know the Word of God.

The way you let the Word of God be the final say so is going over the scripture in 2 Timothy with him or her. In **2 Timothy 2:15**, Paul tells Timothy to "Study to show yourself approved unto God; a workman that needed not to be ashamed but rightly dividing the Word of truth." Show your mentee that it is God's will for us to know the Word of God and to rightly apply it to situations in our lives. Therefore, we all need to have a sound understanding of the Word of

God. You can then inform the mentee that it is the will of the Lord for him or her to study His Word and as a result, needs to incorporate Bible study into his or her personal time. Tell your mentee that God is no respecter of persons; therefore, what He said to Timothy through Paul, He says to us all today. This Word of the Lord will stir a person to do Bible study or to be part of a Bible study group. The best thing about it is that it is not your word but God's Word that gives this directive to the mentee.

- **Accept God's Time Table for the Relationship:**
  It is critical that you and your mentee accept God's time table for your mentoring relationship and to know when to let go when God brings the relationship to an end. This is necessary because when a relationship is ending, you might not understand why, it could be that the mentor or mentee is coming to a new season in his or her life and God wants him or her to be freed up to do the new things that He has for him or her. The Lord can look at the mentee and say OK, he or she can now stand on his or her own so I need to bring some other people to the mentor to raise up. But if the mentor refuses to let go and still continues to hold onto the first mentee and not make room for the next group of people that God has for him or her, what would happen is that the mentor could miss what God has for him or her. Also, if God is trying to move the mentee on to some new things, the mentor can also be hindering the mentee by holding on for too long.

The reverse is also true that if the mentee is holding onto the mentor for too long, the mentee can miss the new thing that God is planning to do in his or her life as well. Therefore, it is good to begin to see and take notice when a relationship is changing. When there seems to be a closure coming, then take it to the Lord and ask for instruction or direction from Him. If it is something that is hard on you because you have become emotionally invested in the person and in the relationship, God can then help you to begin to detach from the person. It does not mean that you will not talk to the person but it might be that you two would no longer communicate as frequently as before but can now talk about once or twice a month. If you examine your life, you will notice that there are some people that you were in a relationship with for a season and it was like everyday you were on the phone together or every other day but now, when you look back, it is like what happened? You sometimes do not even talk to them now but about every three or four months. The reason is because the season for those relationships has changed. Therefore, it is not always healthy to hold on and not let go especially when God is saying to let go of a relationship.

- **Avoid Codependency:**
  This I have said several times before in the previous chapters that codependency is not good. Mentoring sessions are not to become weeping sessions, fix it sessions or emotional sessions about marital issues. As I stated before, if your mentee has emotional issues, refer him or her to where there is professional help. Do not try to be the "fixer-upper" of emotional problems that tend to result in codependency. Refer to Chapter 2 for a discussion on codependence. One of the things that I do not do very well is being codependent. Codependency is a situation in which

you have someone come around you and he or she shares the same story with you over and over again and you give them counsel, godly wisdom and practical solutions but the person never does anything. The person only talks about the problem but never incorporates the solutions. If you do not initially set a boundary in your mentoring relationship, that is, outline the duties of the mentor and the mentee, your mentee might think that he or she is at liberty to call or come over to your house and take you around the mountain with him or her every time the mentee needs a listening ear. The mentee will continue to give you excuses as to why he or she has not done anything about the situation. It is not a good situation to be in when it comes to a mentoring relationship and you as the mentor should not encourage it.

As I stated in the previous chapters, in order for you to avoid codependency, rejection, abandonment and disappointment when the relationship is over, you need to set the duration for the mentoring relationship. It will help you; it will protect you because sometimes you can do things for people and at the end, you come out as the bad guy. Instead of getting a thank you, what you get is a bad report and ungratefulness from the people because they did not understand God's timing for the relationship. This is why it is good for you to set the duration; have a set time for the relationship so that you can tell the person when the time you agreed on is over. You can then let the person know that if God wants the two of you to come back for another season, you will then set another agreed upon time. Do not have an unspecified mentoring time period.

Finally, if you have not prayed with your mentee before to lay hands on him or her, make sure that you do so. Take the time to lay hands on your mentee to release to him or her, those things that the Lord has given you to impart to him or her. God has given you some spiritual gifts and grace that your mentee can benefit from so be willing to release them to your mentee through the laying on of hands. Pray for your mentee or your mentor in your prayer time. I believe that if you are diligent to pay attention to all that is outlined in this book, you will enjoy a very successful mentoring relationship. Are there any questions?

<u>**Note**</u>: *Remember that these materials were first presented in actual classroom settings.*

Question and Answer Session

Gina: What do you do to help a mentee that finds it difficult to make necessary changes after you have spoken extensively with him or her? There might be fear in them in opening up in discussion with the mentor. What do you do to help the mentee?

Mary: I always believe that honesty is the best policy. I do not leave things to assumptions and I do not leave things to chance so when I discern that somebody has been open but there is an area the person is shy or fearful to open up in, my style has always been to ask the person what is going on. I will open the floor for discussion and I will tell the person that I noticed that he or she is not open in this area because it seems to be closed off. I would ask to know the reason why he or she is not open in this area. If it is something that the person does not want to talk about, I will leave the person alone. You cannot force a person to talk about a particular area of their life that they do not want to talk about. All you can do is at least let them know that you are aware of what they think they are masking so well and that their behavior makes the area very transparent to you. You can show your willingness to help the person but the decision to make a move on the matter remains with the person.

If they table the issue for discussion, then you can encourage the person by creating a loving atmosphere for him or her to feel safe. That is why I always tell someone that before you embark on a mentoring relationship make sure it is someone that you can receive from and that it is someone that you can allow to speak into your life. Basically, mentoring is giving permission to someone to speak into your life but that does not mean that the person has to abuse you. Your mentor should be able to hold you accountable and yes, challenge you to grow. Your mentor is working with you to bring out the best in you.

Valerie: You've talked a lot about codependency and how to set up good boundaries from the beginning and how not to get into a codependent relationship. When you see that happening, what are some of the skills that you have established in order to keep people from trying to become codependent on you?

Mary: I think we answered that in one of the previous chapters. I make sure that I do not allow my mentee to take me around the mountain of victimhood and I set boundaries concerning my time. I do hold the mentee accountable for not implementing any of our agreed upon solutions. I told you that I am the type of person that if we have discussed something on more than two occasions and the mentee does not have a valid reason for not taking action, I will tell the mentee that we have talked about this two or three times now and that I am not willing to go around the mountain again with him or her if they are not going to take action. By condoning someone coming and telling you the same story over and over and making the same excuse, you are letting them waste your time and emotion. They are not going anywhere and they want to tie you up also from going anywhere. I cut the person loose after seeking the Lord and the Lord gives me the OK.

Gina: When you have been working with somebody for a while and you have a question about some of the things you see within them, and you are trying to determine if it is something that they need deliverance from or something that is a character issue, how do you know for sure? Obviously you go to the Lord and pray about it, but let's say that you still have some question about exactly what is really going on with the person and what you are dealing with. Can you give me some input in to how to discern that and how to make that decision?

Mary: When you are seeing something about a person and you are trying to access whether it is a character flaw or just a spiritual oppression or something; well, sometimes the oppression could be as a result of the character flaw that brought in the spirit to begin with. It can also be the other way around. For instance, someone who is a chronic liar or a person who has a habit of telling you something and then when you encounter that something it turns out not to be true as they said, can be a person that has a character flaw that needs to be fixed. It might be so chronic to the point that the person might actually need to be delivered from the demon of lying because over the years, the person has given access to the spirit to operate through him or her so the person is now essentially a vessel through which the spirit of untruth operates. All the devil really needs is a little open door in a person's life and he can work on the person to make the door wider.

It will get to a point that the person might not even know when a lie is not necessary. We have encountered some people (ministers) that told us things that were not true and when we come across someone who is also in ministry that knows them, the person will just lay out the truth before us without even knowing that the previous minister had lied about the situation. Some people might need deliverance and some people might just need to fix their character flaws. When the character flaw is fixed, it will shut the door on the devil that has been using it as a legal ground to work through the person to lie.

Also, if you are mentoring someone who is kleptomaniac, the person has a bad habit of picking up things in the stores but he or she might have a strong desire to want to stop but every time he or she goes out there, the demon inspires him or her to pick up something. To the devil, it is a means of control and he enjoys pushing the person's button to make the person steal. This type of person is clearly in need of deliverance because from what you see in their character, he or she is no longer comfortable taking what they used to take in pleasure. Because there is a change in what had been the character flaw, the person can now be delivered from the kleptomaniac spirit so that his or her actions will actually begin to line up with the righteous desire that is now in his or her heart. You see therefore that it all comes down to what is in the heart. Your best indicator is what comes out of the person's heart through their words because the Word of God remains true in **Proverbs 23:7** that:

> **"For as he thinketh in his heart, so is he..."**

Conclusion

In conclusion, I want to give you a quick recap of Chapters 1 through 6 to reinforce what you learned and for those of you that have not read them yet, be sure to study them in detail. I advice you to also read the workbook as well.

Chapter 1: This chapter deals with identifying reasons for needing a mentor or for needing mentoring. You have to be able to articulate to somebody the reasons why you need mentoring or why you think you should be mentoring another person. If the Lord lays it upon your heart, you have to be sure that you get clarification from the Lord that it is Him speaking to you and not your good intentions.

Chapter 2: This chapter talks about selecting a mentor or mentee and I said that it is usually the person who needs mentoring that first seeks the Lord in prayer and looks around in the church to see who would be his or her mentor. There are times that the Lord might lay it upon the heart of someone who is well seasoned in his or her Christian walk to mentor another person. In this case, the person would be the one approaching the would-be-mentee.

Chapter 3: This chapter talks about starting the mentoring relationship. This means understanding the dynamics of a mentoring relationship; what are the things you need to do before you get into this type of relationship? Also, as you step into the relationship, there are some things that you need to make sure that you address. These things are outlined in detail in this chapter so be sure to refer to them in the workbook as well as in this textbook.

Chapter 4: This chapter deals with goal setting and

defining the nature of the mentoring relationship. It is critical to set goals and setup criteria for measuring these goals. You must be able to see at the end of the mentoring relationship if you and your mentee accomplished the stated goals.

Chapter 5: This chapter talks about the act of mentoring; this means the actual mentoring. In other words, what are the things that you do once the mentor and mentee have established a relationship? It outlines in detail how the mentor has to deal with the different issues in the life of the mentee and how the mentor has to help the mentee to develop in his or her Christian growth. It outlines how to mentor men and how to mentor women.

Chapter 6: This chapter deals with how to avoid pitfalls in your mentoring relationship. The reason you need to avoid pitfalls is because in a mentoring relationship, you are working with someone for a season or for a while. You have established a very good relationship with the person and when the relationship comes to a close, or as the relationship is progressing, there are some things that you need to do so that when the season of mentoring in over, you two do not set each other up to feel either rejected or abandoned. You must make sure that the mentee does not feel that you just do not care about him or her anymore. This is why I think that this chapter is necessary because it will help you with your mentee during your relationship and at the end of your relationship. You and your mentee can always make sure that you have the important points discussed in this chapter in the back of your mind so that when the relationship comes to a close, you are aware of the true nature of the relationship that you had.

Mentoring is a very important aspect of the Christian growth and I encourage everyone that is mature or well seasoned in the Lord to seek the Lord so that He can help them to determine who they can impart what they have learned from the Him to. Be willing to mentor and to be mentored. It will help you grow and it will help you to avoid mistakes that other Christians before you have made because you can learn from your mentor how to avoid those mistakes.

Some of the graduating students from the 2007 Mentoring Class

Bibliography

Hamon, Bill, Dr. *Prophets, Pitfalls and Principles: God's Prophetic People Today.* Shippensburg, PA: Destiny Image, 1991.

Joiner, Rick. *The Final Quest.* Charlotte, NC: Morning Star Publications and Ministries, 1997.

Nee, Watchman. *Spiritual Authority.* New York, New York: Christian Fellowship Publishers, Inc., 1972.

Ogenaarekhua, Mary J. *A Workbook for Successful Mentoring.* Atlanta, GA: To His Glory Publishing, Inc., 2007.

Ogenaarekhua, Mary J. *Effective Prayers for Various Situations, Volume 1.* Atlanta, GA: To His Glory Publishing, Inc., 2006.

Ogenaarekhua, Mary J. *How to Discern and Expel Evil Spirits.* Atlanta, GA: To His Glory Publishing, Inc., 2005.

Platz, Ann. *Guardians of the Gate: Enriching Your Life Through Spiritual Mentoring.* Tulsa, OK: Harrison House Inc., 2002.

TO HIS GLORY PUBLISHING COMPANY, INC.

463 Dogwood Dr. Lilburn, GA. 30047, U.S.A (770)458-7947

Order Form for Bookstores in the USA

Order Date: _____

Order Placed By: _____   By Fax: _____

Address: _____

_____

City _____ ST/ZIP _____

Phone #: _____

Email: _____

Purchase Order#: _____

Return Policy: Within 1 year but not before 90 Days.

Price	Quantity	List Price
Shipping Method:		
Media:		
UPS:		
FedEx:		
Other (Please Secify):		
Total Price:	Total Quantity:	List Price

Ship To Address: Bill to Address:

MARY J. MINISTRIES

463 Dogwood Drive, NW
Lilburn, GA 30047
Office 770-458-7947, Fax 770-458-7947

maryjministries@yahoo.com
www.maryjministries.org
Also check
www.tohisglorypublishing
for your publishing needs

Order Form for Books and CDs

Item	Description	Unit Price	Quantity	Total
	Materials by Prophetess Mary J. Ogenaarekhua			
Bk1	Effective Prayers for Various Situations, Vol. I	$16.95		
Bk2	Effective Prayers for Various Situations, Vol. II	$18.95		
Bk3	A Daily Prayer Journal	$10.95		
Bk4	Unveiling the God-mother	$12.95		
Bk5	Keys to Understanding Your Visions and Dreams	$16.95		
Bk6	A Visions and Dreams Journal	$10.95		
Bk7	A Teacher's Manual on Visions and Dreams	$14.95		
Bk8	How to Discern and Expel Evil Spirits	$16.95		
Bk9	A Teachers Manual on Discerning and Expelling Evil Spirits	$14.95		
Bk10	How I Heard From God: The Power of Personal Prophecy	$12.95		
Bk11	Keys to a Successful Mentoring Relationship	$18.95		
Bk12	A Workbook for Successful Mentoring	$14.95		
Bk13	Understanding the Power of Covenant	$19.95		
Bk14	Looking for a Perfect Mate? Qualities of a Godly Man and Woman	$16.95		

CD Sets

Cd1	Visions and Dreams – Six Part Series (Lessons 1-6)	$55.00		
Cd2	How to Discern & Expel Evil Spirits–6 Part Series (Lessons 1-6)	$55.00		

Special Discounts

Set1	SALE-1 of ea. of the 14 books & 1 of ea. of the CD sets (12Cds)	$262.64		

Shipping anywhere in Cont. US: Add $5 for First Item + $2 for Each Additional Item ($20 for Set1 or Set2)

**Please make check or money order
payable to Mary J. Ministries.**

Total of Products Ordered _____
Add 6% Sales Tax _____
Add Shipping & Handling _____
Total with Tax & Shipping _____

For Credit Card Payment *:

Name on Card: _____ Exp Date: _____

Card #:_____ Card Signature: _____
* We accept Visa and MasterCard

Ship Products To:

Name: _____

Address: _____

City: _____ State: _____ Zip:_____

Phone Number _____ Email Address: _____

All Sales Are Final –Contact To His Glory Publishing Co. for Current Prices at 770-458-7947 or tohisglorypublishing@yahoo.com

www.ingramcontent.com/pod-product-compliance
Lightning Source LLC
Chambersburg PA
CBHW070350090426
42733CB00009B/1362